# Secrets From the Master Brewers

America's Top

Professional Brewers

Share Recipes and Tips for

Great Homebrewing

**Patrick Higgins**

**Maura Kate Kilgore**

**Paul Hertlein**

A Fireside Book

Published by Simon & Schuster

FIRESIDE
Rockefeller Center
1230 Avenue of the Americas
New York, NY 10020

Designed by Barbara M. Bachman

Manufactured in the United States of America

1 3 5 7 9 10 8 6 4 2

Library of Congress Cataloging-in-Publication Data

Higgins, Patrick.
Secrets from the master brewers: America's top professional
brewers share recipes and tips for great homebrewing/ Patrick
Higgins, Maura Kate Kilgore, Paul Hertlein.
p. cm.
"A Fireside book."
Includes index.
1. Brewing—Amateur's manuals. I. Kilgore, Maura Kate.
II. Hertlein, Paul. III. Title.
TP570.H544 1998
641.8'73—dc21 98-26353
CIP

ISBN 0-684-84190-8 (alk. paper)

*To our Family and Friends,*

*Who gave us the confidence*

*to put our dreams ahead of our expectations*

# ACKNOWLEDGMENTS

*Special thanks to all of the brewers who contributed their time and knowledge to this project — not only those featured in chapters of their own, but the countless others whose insights, though no less enlightening, could not be featured due to the limitations of time and space. We learned a lot from you all, and made some good friends along the way.*

*Thanks also to our friends in the brewing community who went out of their way to help us locate a national selection of top-notch homebrewers-turned pro. Sebbie Buehler, Mark Silva and Paul Sayler all deserve special thanks in this department.*

*Thanks also to Becky Cabaza and Dan Lane at Fireside, whose patience with this unwieldy project was never-ending.*

*And of course, love and thanks to Philip Spitzer, who made it all happen for us.*

# CONTENTS

# INTRODUCTION

They were a fiction writer, a bartender, a CAD designer, a chef, a pharmacist, a mechanical engineer, a photo lab worker. In their off-hours, they all shared one passion — homebrewing. Eventually they all made their passion their profession.

Do you remember the first taste of your first homebrew? The cautious enthusiasm as you poured it into its glass, and took in its perfect color and sturdy head. The lilt of your eyebrows as you inhaled its delicious aroma and realized that you couldn't wait to taste it. And, finally, your broad grin as you experienced for the first time the fine balance of hops and malt, the bursting bubbles of good carbonation. Success. Epiphany.

And so the passion for homebrewing is born. It is a passion rooted in the love of good beer. It is a passion that embraces the creativity of the culinary arts. It is a passion that revels in the intellectual challenges of biology, chemistry, and engineering presented by each batch. Above all, it is a passion for the simple satisfaction of handcrafting a good beer.

And once the passion has ensnared us, we are defenseless against its powers. We find ourselves spending our money on bigger and better equipment, turning previously quiet corners of our homes into breweries, and deserting our families and friends to pursue our passion. (At least we share it when we're done, right?) And who among us has not dreamed of turning this passion into a career? After all, isn't making money doing something you love the real American dream?

*Secrets From the Master Brewers* is in its own way a master class. It's a chance to sit down with some of the finest brewers in America and have them share the little things they have learned as professionals—little things that will make better beer. They have also shared many of their own recipes, some of which have earned medals at the Great American Beer Festival. Every ingredient listed and every technique used in these recipes is something you can do at home. There really aren't any "secrets," but simply the right choice of ingredients, blended in the right proportions, utilized in the best way.

A few years ago, these professionals were just like you—lovers of great beer arduously pursuing their hobby in their kitchens and basements. Perhaps they will inspire you to follow your dream and become a professional brewer. Certainly, they will give you new insights and tips to make your homebrew as good as it can possibly be. "But," you might say, "there are certain things that I simply can't do at home." Well, then, maybe you should become a pro. There is always room in the world for more great beer.

# PROLOGUE
## HOMEBREWING—CONSENSUS AND DEBATE

In brewing, there are often many paths to the same outcome, and brewers are passionate about which method works best for them. From choice of ingredients to mashing techniques, battles rage. And yet as we interviewed this varied group of brewers from around the United States, we noticed that there were many questions to which we repeatedly received similar answers.

Of course, there was never complete agreement on anything, which leads us to the debates. As usual, the debates were a little harder to handle, but no matter what our opinion, we emerged wiser as a result. We hope you will too.

### CONSENSUS

#### *Hops*

The majority of brewers expressed a strong general preference for pellet hops. Most agreed that in a perfect world, whole-leaf hops would be ideal. "They're closer to the source," explains Paul Sayler, of New York's Commonwealth Brewery (although, like several other brewers, he uses pellets due to system limitations). Whole-leaf hops, however, don't exhibit the stability of pellets in storage, especially imported varieties, which are not handled as efficiently as American hops. "Pellets are easier to dispose of, easier to weigh, they store better, and they're more consistent," sums up Pacific Coast's Don Gortemiller.

Many, like Elysian's Dick Cantwell and Buffalo Bill's Bill Owens, use pellets for all phases. ("I can't mess with leaves," quips Bill.) As Ray McNeill, of McNeill's Pub and Brewery, explains, "Whole flowers don't get thoroughly immersed in the dry hop. They just float on top. I tried weighting them, but it's just easier to use pellets."

A subgroup, however, prefers to indulge in the integrity of flower hops for aroma and dry hopping. Pike Place's Fal Allen dry-hops using plugs, placing them in muslin hop bags and adding them to the conditioned beer. Dan Rogers, of Holy Cow! Brewpub and Casino, uses flowers in a hop back designed specifically for them. Keith Villa, of Blue Moon Brewing Company, predicts a rise in the use of hop oils, because their quality has increased recently. "Oils are really the most stable form of hops. The Germans use them a lot."

### Water Treatment

Few of the brewers we spoke to tinkered much with their brewing water, and very few advocated water treatment on the homebrewing level. "If you can drink it, you can pretty much brew with it," says Don Gortemiller. Quite a few suggested getting a water profile, available from your local water company. If your water comes from a well, you can buy an inexpensive water test kit at any hardware store that will measure the elements you're interested in. Check for chlorine levels (boil or filter if not less than 0.1 ppm), mineral content, and pH. Compare these to the chart in Greg Noonan's *The New Brewing Lager Beer* to determine how to replicate water sources around the world.

Most breweries use filtered water, so they know that their water falls within acceptable profiles, and they adjust with chemicals only when necessary for style. "Pilsners need soft water. Homebrewers should use bottled spring water," suggests Keith Villa. British styles require hard water, and most brewers add calcium carbonate (gypsum) to the mash. "Soft water is warmer and maltier," explains Nick Hankin, of Highlander Brewery and Real Ale Consulting. "Hard water is drier." Several brewers also encourage the use of calcium carbonate when brewing with dark malts. "Dark malts are acidic and can contribute a burnt taste. Calcium carbonate makes the water less acidic and mellows those flavors," says Keith Villa.

The few dissidents who do treat their brewing water do so for reasons closely linked to their brewing styles. Michael Ferguson, of Gordon Biersch, uses reverse osmosis, then adds minerals and salts to establish a soft water profile appropriate for the Bavarian styles he brews at Barley's Brewpub and Casino. Nick Hankin and brewing partner Luca Evans re-created the water of Glasgow for their authentic Scottish styles. Ever the chef, Heartland Brewery's Jim Migliorini makes the unusual addition of salt (NaCl): "For flavor, baby! It also keeps the yeast in check, on a certain level."

On the flip side, a few brewers prefer not to replicate authentic styles but to create their own take on a style, and they can do that by retaining their local water profile. "Using your own water lets a local character show through," advocates Don Gortemiller. Greg Noonan advises brewing styles that suit your water: "If you have hard water, brew hoppy beers. If you have soft water, brew dark beers."

### Full, Rolling Boils

The beauty and utility of a really good boil was a subject that inspired discussion in almost romantic terms for many of the brewers. Drew Cluley, of Pyramid Brewing Company and his own consultancy, speaks in galactic terms of a good protein break. Ray McNeill is emphatic that a boil must be both long and hard: "Sixty minutes is too short. You get better hop utilization, proteins drop out better, and you drive off more DMS [dimethyl sulfide]," he insists. In fact, most of the brewers we spoke to boiled for at least 90 minutes. Increasing this time is recommended for maltier beers, where a caramel character is desired. Drew Cluley boils his Scotch ale for 3 hours, "to really get those melanoidins developing." Melanoidins, derived from specialty malts, contribute about two-thirds of wort color during boiling.

When it comes to sanitation, you can't be too careful. Almost every brewer mentioned sanitation, and our visits to their breweries often exposed just how seriously sanitation is taken on the professional level. At Barley's, Michael Ferguson requires treading through a pan of iodophor solution upon entering the brewery. Our friend Sadie, who had unfortunately chosen open shoes for the visit, had to wrap her feet in plastic bags. "Sanitation is 70 percent of what we do," Michael explains.

## DEBATE

### *Grain*

A complex question encompassing a range of issues, there is little accord among brewers as to the best grain. The choice is more than just a matter of taste, which in itself is enough to provoke strongly opinionated reactions, but also a question of efficiency, availability, and style.

For starters, there's the age-old debate over two-row versus six-row malt. Two-row malt has a higher starch-to-husk ratio, while six-row is less expensive. Especially for smaller breweries, the savings in using six-row don't make up for the trade-offs. "There's very little starch and lots of husk," explains Ray McNeill. "The result is a phenolic, astringent character." In fact, almost all of the brewers we spoke to use two-row. A notable exception is the addition of up to 50 percent six-row malt for beers with a large percentage of wheat, rye, or other grains lacking enzymatic power. "Six-row has higher enzymatic power than two-row," pronounces Dan Rogers. However, several did question whether there really is a discernible difference in the finished product. "I'd like to see anyone tell the difference in a blind taste test. There's no difference," states Bill Owens.

Do regional styles require the use of grains from that region? Many brewers said yes. According to Fal Allen, "If you want the flavors of a region, use the hops and grains from there." Why? "Those grains were developed over hundreds of years for use in those beers," explains Luca Evans. Of course, not everyone agreed. "It's important if you're shooting for traditional character, but it also depends on style," clarifies Paul Sayler. "In a porter, for example, it's less important." Michael Ferguson believes that use of regional grains is not necessary because they may be modified differently. "The familiar can be better used," he says, but he does cite several styles that are defined by their malt bill: "A pilsner needs Cara-Pils; a Märzen needs Munich." Others, like Jim Migliorini, question the results. "Without the same water, same system, et cetera, there's no point," he pronounces. (An aside: When it comes to brewing with extracts, use extracts that are produced as locally as possible. Imported extracts are more concentrated and can be darker and possess a more caramelized quality.)

Creating a grain bill is truly a personal thing, we quickly discovered. Based almost purely on taste, the choice of emphasizing a single grain or blending a variety of malts saw little accord. "Use as many as you can that are appropriate to the style. You'll get more malt character," pronounces Nick Hankin on one side of the debate. In agreement, Paul Sayler offers, "I get a more complex character with a blend. I don't want one ingredient to stand out above the others." On the flip side, Fal Allen asserts, "Simple is better for malt bills. Blending muddies the flavors." And Jim Migliorini seems shocked by the very notion of blending malts: "No!" he exclaims. "That would hide the identity of the individual malts." Still others straddle the fence, using a limited number, like Drew Cluley, who routinely incorporates three to five grains in his beers.

What is a true porter, and what is a true stout? Since the origin of the porter style is somewhat debatable, no one can be sure what characteristics define a true porter. The tendency has been to define stouts by a dominance of roasted barley and porters by a dominance of chocolate malt.

## *Mashing*

Mash techniques vary widely from brewer to brewer, encompassing a wide range of temperatures, schedules, and methods. The biggest debates are about mashing techniques and the length of the mash.

Decoction mashing, once used to obtain greater yields from undermodified malts, is still favored by some, although no longer necessary. "As a homebrewer, I always double-decocted," asserts Dick Cantwell. Paul Sayler feels that decoction is worth the time, but warns that results vary with malt and equipment. "It really requires a lot of trial and error," advises Paul. "For decoction to work, you need malts that work and a system that works. Play around with different pots, different heat sources."

If you are committed to trying decoction, choose an appropriate style, such as Märzen or Doppelbock, and appropriate malt. Brewers of German-style lagers are adamant about the need for decoction mashing for these beers. "It gives it that signature nutty flavor," explains Keith Villa.

For many, the extra effort isn't warranted by the subtle results. "Why bother?" opines Bill Owens. "There's a 1 percent difference at best." And, in fact, most of the brewers we interviewed use single-infusion mashing. One reason is that it is the simplest method, and most effective for basic ale production. Ray McNeill described his experience with decoction as a nightmare: "We're not set up to do decoction. Back when I used to do it, it was all manual. Manual firing of the mash, manually moving this boiling shit around!" Bob Johnson, from Magic Hat Brewing Company in Burlington, Vermont, also uses single infusion at the production level, just as he did at home. "I tried doing protein rests when I made some wheat beers, but who knows if it worked. I don't think you can get the necessary control on the stovetop." Bob suggests investing in a decent insulated mash tun for all-grain brews to achieve control of single-infusion mash temperatures.

The length of the mash rest is another issue that most brewers do not agree on. Dick Cantwell mashed for 90 minutes as a homebrewer, but as a professional, he shortened it to 60 minutes at both Big Time and Pike Place. Rogue's John Maier feels that "extended mash temperatures are unnecessary with today's well-modified malts." Bob Johnson has done conversion checks at Magic Hat and discovered that the majority of his mashes are fully converted in 45 minutes. There was frequent mention among the brewers we spoke to of one West Coast brewer who performs a notorious 10-minute mash, and studies indicate that this might indeed be long enough for full starch conversion, given the right water-to-malt ratio.

All things considered, the larger the mash is, the more uniform your temperature and water distribution will be, and the more efficiently starch conversion will occur. Most homebrewers will not achieve complete conversion in less than 60 to 90 minutes. Check for conversion with iodine, and when in doubt, let it rest longer. You cannot overconvert your mash.

Greg Noonan employs step infusion and decoction at the Vermont Pub and Brewery and the Seven Barrel Brewpub, depending on the style of beer being brewed. On the homebrew level, you have the flexibility of working with small quantities. If you can fit your mash tun on your stovetop, you can do step-infusion mashing. Paul Sayler tells us that step infusion helps reduce chill haze by reducing large protein particles during a 15-minute protein rest at 125° to 130°F.

No matter what your technique is, Greg Noonan warns that hot side aeration can occur in the mash. "A lot of brewers don't think much about splashing mash around, impacting air into the mash. You'll end up with astringency in the beer, every beer, all the time."

# 1.

## KEITH VILLA

### Blue Moon Brewing Company/Coors

*"I had to ask myself if I wanted to work with sick people or beer. I chose beer."*

**K**eith Villa began homebrewing in 1983 while studying molecular biology at the University of Colorado at Boulder, in preparation for a career in medicine. He was headed to the University of Colorado Medical School, when he was presented with a more tempting option. Coors Brewing Company happened to be looking for someone to do research in fermentation sciences, something that Keith had done during his junior and senior years.

Keith worked at Coors for two years and then decided to pursue his doctorate. He attended the University of Brussels in Belgium, receiving a Ph.D. in brewing and fermentation biochemistry—making him one of only a handful of brewers in America to hold a Ph.D. in the field. While abroad, he traveled and researched beer extensively throughout Europe, learning different styles and brewing techniques.

Upon his return, he assumed the role of master brewer at the Blue Moon Brewing Company, one of few American breweries featuring Belgian-style ales. Since then, he has garnered numerous medals, including a gold medal for his Belgian White Ale at the 1995 World Beer Championships. Keith is a certified beer judge and judges annually at the Great American Beer Festival.

## BREWING BELGIAN ALES

Keith's experience and education make him an authority on Belgian styles, a topic that intrigues many homebrewers. Belgian-style ales are among the most difficult beers to replicate—not only because of the unique yeast strains, which have been cultivated over hundreds of years by hundreds of breweries, but also the unique Belgian approach to beer. Unlike their stoic German neighbors, Keith says that Belgians will add anything to beer: unmalted wheat, oats, rice, corn, orange peel, coriander, corn syrup, candy sugar, and even saccharine—not to mention the synergy of bacteria and wild yeast in one of their most popular styles, lambic. Belgian whites, abbey dubbels, trippels, and lambics each offers its own challenges for recipe formulation and brewing technique.

### Belgian White Ales

Belgian White (*wit* in Flemish) was one of the first styles Keith introduced at Blue Moon. Belgian whites are wheat ales with a light, creamy texture and a refreshing citrus quality. Recipes should include at least 50 percent two-row pale malt, 30 to 40 percent unmalted wheat, and, to achieve the creamy texture, up to 10 percent rolled oats. "Contemporary Belgian brewers avoid oats because they aid in clarification, diminishing the signature cloudiness," Keith explains, "but I consider oats essential to the style." Original gravity between 1.045 and 1.050 (11–12.5° Plato) with alcohol content of 5.0 to 5.5 percent by volume is appropriate.

Hopping rates are low (15–25 IBUs—International Bitterness Units) and traditionally of the noble varieties, such as Tettnanger,

Hallertauer, or Saaz. Use of aroma hops is minimal because the Belgian white derives its characteristic aromatics from the addition of curaçao orange peel and coriander in the brew kettle.

More important than the malt and hop varieties is the strain of yeast. Keith insists that in any beer, it is the yeast that adds the distinctive notes that define the style. "You can't add orange and coriander to a beer fermented with just any ale yeast and expect to get an authentic Belgian white." Belgian white yeast is readily available in homebrew supply shops.

### Abbey-Style Ales

Belgian Abbey–style ales, such as dubbels and trippels, have been brewed in monasteries for centuries. Each brewery has developed its own distinctive flavor, largely due to the use of proprietary yeast strains. Common to both dubbels and trippels is a rich, malty character accompanied by assertive flavors from the yeast. These beers are typically strong (unlike singles brewed for the monks' own consumption) and medium bodied. To achieve this combination, abbey beers are brewed using 10 to 30 percent candy sugar. However, Belgian brewers use a syrup that is more closely approximated by corn syrup than the rock candy–like sugar commonly available from homebrew suppliers. Dubbels are darker in color, so dark corn syrup should be used; trippels should be as light in color as possible, so light corn syrup is appropriate.

Keith recommends the use of small quantities of Cara-Pils malt in trippels because "it contributes a full, malty flavor without the burned taste of darker, roasted malts." An addition of 3 to 8 percent of Special B malt is essential to achieve the prune/raisin character in dubbels. The balance of the grain bill consists of two-row pale malt. Original gravity varies widely among Belgian breweries. Dubbels are typically between 1.050 and 1.070 (12.5–17.5° Plato) with alcohol content of 6.0 to 7.5 percent by volume, and trippels are typically between 1.060 and 1.095 (17.5–24° Plato) with an alcohol content of 7 to 10 percent by volume.

Hopping rates should be low, since the malt is the focus for these styles; 10 to 20 IBUs are necessary for balance. Very little aroma hops should be added. If you are particularly fond of Orval, dry-hop with 10 to 15 percent of your total hop bill; it is the only Trappist that uses this technique.

The proper yeast strain is the key to creating an authentic abbey beer. You could risk eternal damnation and sneak into an abbey brewery to steal a yeast culture, but it's simpler to buy a Belgian abbey culture. Another option is to cultivate a sample from a bottle-conditioned abbey beer. Keith warns, however, that the yeast found at the bottom of the bottle is often a second strain added at the conditioning phase—typically a lager strain, used to ensure maximum flocculation during conditioning, and not the ale strain used in primary fermentation, where the distinctive esters are produced. Some brewers add a second yeast strain or additional sugars during secondary fermentation to ensure maximum attenuation of these strong beers.

### Lambics

Lambics are the true enigma of Belgian beers. Their mouth-puckering complexities are mainly attributable to the spontaneous fermentation by wild yeast found only in the Senne Valley. Keith warns, "Don't try experimenting with your local microorganisms that happen to be in the air."

The best a homebrewer can do is approximate this complex process. Lambic fermentation begins when the hot wort is pumped into large, shallow vats, either on the roof or close to the roof of the brewery. As it cools overnight, the wort is inoculated with a variety of microflora. It's then transferred into large oak barrels, where it ferments. Initially the bacteria in the wort grow at a faster pace than the yeast, contributing the unusual flavors that are the hallmark of lambics. Eventually the yeast produces enough ethanol to kill off *Escherichia coli* and other bacteria. Lactobacillus remains, continuing to produce lactic acid, which is eventually esterified into ethyl lactate—the source of the distinguishing aroma of lambics. The struggle for food eventually results in the demise of the lactobacillus as the *Brettanomyces lambicus* and *B. bruxelliensis* yeast dominate.

In an effort to re-create this beer at home, it is best to purchase a *B. lambicus/B. bruxelliensis* yeast culture, which also contains a lactobacillus culture (available from Wyeast). Additional lactic acid can be added midway through primary fermentation, giving it sufficient time to become esterified. Another option, suggested in *The Homebrewer's Recipe Guide*, is a full wort sour, accomplished by adding a small amount of crushed pale malt to 120°F wort prior to fermentation. Then, the wort must be soured for a week to achieve sufficient lactobacillus content.

A small amount of old, stale hops added to the boil helps keep the bacteria in check during fermentation without adding bitterness. Add 10 IBUs based on the original alpha acid content of the hops when fresh. No aroma hops should be added.

The grain bill for a lambic should be 30 to 50 percent unmalted wheat, and the balance two-row pale malt. Many brewers add unfermentable sugars or other sweeteners like saccharine to the boil to offset the tart flavors.

To produce fruit lambics, perhaps the most popular of the lambic styles, add pasteurized fruit during secondary fermentation for 7 to 10 days. Although cherry (kreik) and raspberry (framboise) are most common, virtually any fruit can be added. Commercial varieties include everything from peaches to bananas to plums. (For guidelines on adding fruit to beer, see Jim Migliorini, Chapter 9.)

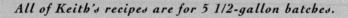

*All of Keith's recipes are for 5 1/2-gallon batches.*

# BELGIAN WIT

5 POUNDS 2-ROW PALE MALT

2 3/4 POUNDS UNMALTED WHITE WHEAT

1 POUND ROLLED OATS

1 OUNCE HALLERTAUER HOPS, 3.5% ALPHA

1/4 OUNCE SAAZ HOPS, 2.6% ALPHA

1/2 OUNCE BITTER ORANGE PEEL

1 1/4 OUNCES GROUND CORIANDER

WYEAST WITBEER YEAST 3944

1 CUP CORN SUGAR (TO PRIME)

OG: 1.049 • FG: 1.008

Mash in at 42°C and hold for 20 minutes. Raise to 50°C and hold for 25 minutes. Raise to 66°C and hold for 60 minutes. Raise to 75°C and hold for 10 minutes and mash out. Boil for 90 minutes, adding Hallertauer hops after 15 minutes and Saaz hops after 60 minutes. Add orange peel and coriander during the final 5 minutes of the boil. Cool wort and pitch yeast. Ferment 5 to 7 days. Transfer to a secondary fermenter, and ferment an additional 5 days. Keg or bottle with corn sugar. Age 5 to 7 days before serving.

# DUBBEL

9 3/4 POUNDS 2-ROW PALE MALT

1 POUND SPECIAL B (DEWOLF-COSYNS)

1 1/4 POUNDS DARK CORN SYRUP

2 1/4 OUNCES STYRIAN GOLDINGS HOPS, 2.3% ALPHA

1 OUNCE SAAZ HOPS, 2.6% ALPHA

WYEAST ABBEY YEAST 1214

3/4 CUP CORN SUGAR (TO PRIME)

OG: 1.063 • FG: 1.011

Mash in at 50°C and hold for 20 minutes. Raise to 66°C and hold for 45 minutes. Raise to 75°C and hold for 10 minutes and mash out. Boil for 90 minutes, adding Styrian Goldings hop when wort reaches boil. After 30 minutes, cool wort and pitch yeast. Ferment 5 to 7 days at 68–70°C. Transfer to a secondary fermenter, and ferment an additional 5 days. Keg or bottle with corn sugar. Age 5 to 7 days before serving.

# TRIPPEL

12 3/4 POUNDS 2-ROW PALE MALT

3/4 POUND CARA-PILS MALT (DEWOLF-COSYNS)

2 1/3 POUNDS LIGHT CORN SYRUP

3/4 OUNCE HALLERTAUER HOPS, 6.4% ALPHA

1/4 OUNCE HALLERTAUER HOPS, 6.4% ALPHA

WYEAST ABBEY YEAST 1762

3/4 CUP CORN SUGAR (TO PRIME)

OG: 1.083 • FG: 1.010

Mash in at 40°C and hold for 20 minutes. Raise to 52°C and hold for 30 minutes. Raise to 66°C and hold for 45 minutes. Raise to 75°C and hold for 10 minutes and mash out. Boil for 90 minutes, adding 3/4 ounce Hallertauer hops when wort reaches a boil. After 20 minutes, add 1/4 ounce Hallertauer hops. Cool wort and pitch yeast. Ferment 5 to 7 days. Transfer to a secondary fermenter, and ferment an additional 5 days. Keg or bottle with corn sugar. Age 5 to 7 days before serving.

# GUEUZE

5 POUNDS 2-ROW PALE MALT

3 1/2 POUNDS UNMALTED WHITE WHEAT

3/4 OUNCE HALLERTAUER HOPS, 3.5% ALPHA

WYEAST BELGIAN LAMBIC BLEND 3278

3/4 CUP CORN SUGAR (TO PRIME)

OG: 1.048 • FG: 1.008

Mash in at 42°C and hold for 20 minutes. Raise to 50°C and hold for 25 minutes. Raise to 66°C and hold for 60 minutes. Raise to 75°C, hold for 10 minutes, and mash out. Boil for 90 minutes, adding 3/4 ounce Hallertauer hops when wort reaches a boil. Cool wort and pitch yeast. Ferment 5 to 7 days. Transfer to a secondary fermenter, and ferment an additional 21 to 28 days. Keg or bottle with corn sugar. Age a minimum of 6 months before serving.

# 2

# MICHAEL FERGUSON

*Gordon Biersch/Barley's Brewpub and Casino*

*"Every aspect of making Bavarian lagers is important. It's been done that way for years, and it shouldn't change now."*

**B**efore he became a professional brewer, Michael Ferguson worked as a mechanical engineer at IBM for 12 years. His experience with the precision and exacting standards required by engineering shows amply in his Bavarian lagers, brewed in the best of German traditions—not what you'd expect from Michael's easygoing but spirited presence.

Michael first dabbled with homebrewing in high school, then took it up more seriously in 1983. The Gordon Biersch chain offered Michael an opportunity for a career change, and he jumped at it. He now serves as the regional brewer for Gordon Biersch and oversees a number of its breweries. Henderson, Nevada, serves as his home base, where he produces some of the finest Bavarian lagers in the country.

Precision and tradition are the overriding themes in brewing Bavarian lagers. These beers have been brewed the same way for centuries (except, of course, for innovations in equipment). This tradition and precision begins with the brewing ingredients.

It is impossible to discuss the grain bill for Bavarian lagers without discussing the mash. These beers are traditionally decocted, a time-consuming process necessary with the undermodified malts of earlier brewing ages. Decoction results in a signature flavor that has become a stylistic hallmark of German lagers. German malts continue to be modified for decocting. Although Michael doesn't believe it is necessary to use German malts for these styles, and in fact uses American two-row at Barley's, he does counsel, "If you use German malt, you must decoct. If you don't want to take the time to decoct, don't use German malt." Michael also warns, "Avoid Breiss malt for lagers. It just doesn't work well, and when you decoct it, it gets even worse."

Michael insists on two-row malt because it provides a better base for lagers than six-row malt. "It has better proteins, and attenuates better." And, of course, the Reinheitsgebot requires that no adjuncts or sugars be used at any time in the brewing process.

Each style demands specific grains. "You can't brew a Märzen without Munich malt. A pilsner needs Cara-Pils. A dunkel must have dark wheat—not a pale wheat darkened with another grain," explains Michael. He also prefers slow-roasted German Weyermann or Bamburg dark malts, finding the American black malts to have a burned quality. Belgian Carastan has replaced caramel malts in many of Michael's recipes: "I love that malt in anything copper colored or beyond."

Noble hops are used exclusively. The European character of these hops furnishes the signature flavor for Bavarian lagers. For the most part, noble hops are interchangeable, and no particular variety is required for a particular style. However, Michael recommends Spalt and Saaz for light beers like pilsners. "Spalt and Saaz are very sharp and spicy. I think they fight the dark malts." Noble varieties blend well, and traditional lagers may feature two or three varieties.

Precision and tradition are essential in the process. Even when working with highly modified malts, all Bavarian lagers should be decocted to provide the authentic flavor. When doing a single decoction, mash in all grain for 30 minutes. Remove the thickest one-third of the mash, and add to a pot. Add a small amount of water, and boil for 15 minutes. Cool to 155°F and add back to mash tun and remix. Stabilize to 168°F for 30 minutes and mash out. Bigger beers like bocks and double bocks should always be double-decocted. To double-decoct, follow the above steps until remixing the mash. At this point, let it rest for 15 minutes. Again remove the thickest one-third of the mash, and add to a pot. Add a small amount of water, and boil for 15 minutes. Cool to 155°F, add back to the mash tun, and remix. Stabilize to 168°F for 30 minutes, and mash out. To triple-decoct, repeat the process once again.

The fermentation process is the key to all lagers, including Bavarian styles. Michael suggests stepping up lager yeast at least twice before pitching. The wort must be at least 40°F before pitching. Never cheat and pitch the yeast at a warmer temperature to get it going quickly. But also never allow the wort to cool down past 33°F. "Pitching at colder temperatures will cause the yeast to sweat less, which can contribute some harsh flavors," Michael advises. Get your beer going quickly by aerating it. (Michael says, "Aerate the hell out of it.") Let the wort rise naturally to a maximum of 48–50°F. Ferment for 7 days, and then drop the temperature to 40°F.

If you plan to harvest yeast for repitching, harvest at this point. Transfer to a secondary fermenter, and let the beer rise to 51°F for 3 days. This warmer temperature will allow the yeast to reabsorb elements that contribute harsh flavors. For this reason, never repitch lager yeast from a secondary fermenter.

After 3 days, begin the conditioning or lagering phase. Bring the temperature down slowly to as close to 32°F as you can (as slowly as

1°F a day if possible). Don't crash-cool, or you might shock the yeast and cause much of it to go dormant. Step cooling produces a much smoother, cleaner beer. "Even lager yeast will produce esters above what they should at warmer temperatures, so if you want to smooth the beer out, you'll do slow temperature processing."

All Bavarian lagers should be conditioned a minimum of 3 weeks, 4 weeks is better, and 6 weeks is optimum. Bocks and double bocks should be conditioned for 2 to 3 months.

Michael believes cleanliness and sanitation are the biggest key to being a successful brewer, regardless of the style you're making. "Sanitation is 70 percent of what you do. Don't skimp. Don't cut corners."

# HELL

### Light Lager

5 POUNDS PALE 2-ROW MALT

2.6 POUNDS MALTED WHITE WHEAT

.80 OUNCE HALLERTAUER HERSBRUCKER HOPS, 3.9% ALPHA

.15 OUNCE SAAZ HOPS, 3.9% ALPHA

GERMAN LAGER YEAST

Mash in grains at 125.5°F and hold for 20 minutes. Raise temperature to 144° and hold for 20 minutes. Raise temperature to 154°F and hold for 20 minutes. Raise temperature to 162°F and hold for 30 minutes. Mash out at 172°F. Bring wort to a boil and add Hallertauer Hersbrucker hops. Boil for 90 minutes. Turn off heat and add Saaz hops. Let steep while whirlpooling wort to drop out solids. Cool wort and pitch yeast. Lager as instructed in previous chapter.

# VIENNA VELVET

5 POUNDS PALE 2-ROW MALT

.48 POUND CARA-PILS

3.5 POUNDS MUNICH MALT (90L)

1.15 OUNCES HALLERTAUER HERSBRUCKER HOPS, 3.9% ALPHA

GERMAN LAGER YEAST

Mash in grains at 125.5°F and hold for 20 minutes. Raise temperature to 144°F and hold for 20 minutes. Raise temperature to 154°F and hold for 20 minutes. Raise temperature to 162°F and hold for 30 minutes. Mash out at 172°F. Bring wort to a boil and add one ounce Hallertauer Hersbrucker hops. Boil for 90 minutes. Turn off heat and add .15 ounce Hallertauer Hersbrucker hops. Let steep while whirlpooling wort to drop out solids. Cool wort and pitch yeast. Lager as instructed in previous chapter.

In addition to handling the brewing at Barley's Casino and Brewing Company in Las Vegas, Michael also oversees the brewing for the other Gordon Biersch facilities around the country. The following two recipes are from his brewer Michael Snyder in Kansas City, who brews at Hofbrauhaus Brewery and Biergarten and Station Casino. Michael felt they would make great additions to the book.

## DOUBLE MADURO STOUT

### West Coast Stout

9.45 POUNDS PALE 2-ROW MALT

1/8 POUND CHOCOLATE MALT

.45 POUND CARA-PILS MALT

.65 POUND CRYSTAL MALT (40L)

.90 POUND FLAKED BARLEY

.65 POUND ROASTED BARLEY

1.25 OUNCES WHEAT MALT

.50 POUND ROLLED OATS

1.4 OUNCES WILLAMETTE HOPS, 5.3% ALPHA

1.3 OUNCES EAST KENT GOLDINGS HOPS, 4.5% ALPHA

.50 OUNCE MT. HOOD HOPS, 5.5% ALPHA

.50 OUNCE CASCADE HOPS, 5% ALPHA

WYEAST 1056 LIQUID YEAST CULTURE

### OG: 12 PLATO

Mash grains at 158°F. Sparge and collect wort. Bring wort to a boil and add Willamette and East Kent Goldings hops. Boil for 90 minutes, adding Mt. Hood hops after 60 minutes and Cascade hops after 85 minutes. Cool wort to 60°F and pitch yeast. Ferment for 6 days. Raise temperature to 72°F and ferment an additional 2 to 3 days. Drop temperature to 32.5°F as quickly as possible and let rest 4 to 5 days. Transfer to secondary fermenter. Bottle or keg.

# WILD RICE PALE ALE

9 POUNDS PALE 2-ROW MALT

.60 POUND BISCUIT MALT

.65 POUND CRYSTAL MALT (40L)

.60 POUND MUNICH MALT (10L)

1 POUND LONG GRAIN WILD RICE

.35 OUNCE CLUSTER HOPS, 7% ALPHA

1 OUNCE TETTNANGER HOPS, 5.5% ALPHA

.35 OUNCE EAST KENT GOLDINGS HOPS, 4.5% ALPHA

WYEAST 1056 LIQUID YEAST CULTURE

## OG: 13.5 PLATO

Mash grains at 158°F for 60 minutes. Boil wild rice in 1.5 quarts of water to gelatinize starches. Add rice to mash, raising the temperature to 168°F. Sparge and collect wort. Bring wort to a boil and add cluster hops. Boil for 90 minutes, adding Tettnanger hops after 60 minutes and East Kent Goldings hops after 85 minutes. Cool wort to 70°F and pitch yeast. Ferment for 6 days. Drop temperature to 32.5°F as quickly as possible and let rest for 3 days. Transfer to secondary fermenter. Bottle or keg.

# 3.

## DREW CLULEY

### Pyramid Brewing Company

*"I really like to see that protein break. You get that kind of 'warping into a star field.' If you look down into the kettle, it looks like the Millennium Falcon just went into warp drive."*

**D**rew Cluley's unabashed enthusiasm for brewing dates back to 1990, when his sister gave him Dave Miller's *The Complete Handbook of Home Brewing* as a birthday gift. Drew soon found himself hooked.

In 1993, after being laid off from his job on the East Coast, he moved to Seattle (where his sister lives) in search of a job in the brewing industry. With Bill Jenkins, a brewer at Pike Brewery in Seattle and later a Great American Beer Festival gold medal winner at Big Time in Seattle (and now his brother-in-law), Drew continued to pursue his passion for homebrewing, eventually creating a homebrewing system that is unparalleled in our experience (you should see this basement!).

In 1994, Drew learned that Pyramid would be building a new brewery in Seattle. Armed with a resumé and three bottles of homebrew (one of them a banana beer, which is included here), he went in search of a job. Three days later, he was one of four brewers at the new Pyramid Brewing Company in Seattle.

Drew worked for two years at Pyramid Brewing Company, brewing both the Pyramid and Thomas Kemper products before moving on to form his own brewing consultancy business, which has taken him as far as Japan in the never-ending mission to teach others to brew good beer. Drew continues to work at Pyramid, though now helping out the sales and marketing department more than working in the brewery. He also maintains his consulting business. One of his primary functions as a consultant is that of recipe formulation, and Drew continues to create and refine professional recipes on his incredible basement system.

## RECIPE FORMULATION

The first step in formulating a great recipe is deciding on your beer's profile. Are you attempting to brew a classic style? Are you attempting to simulate a commercial product? Or are you trying to create your own signature brew? Whatever the goal, carefully analyze the qualities you want in your finished product. Taste, appearance, aroma, body, and alcohol content are all determined by your recipe. Visualize your beer, and analyze its properties.

Designating original and finishing gravities is the first step in determining the contents of your grain bill. If you are brewing a classic style, consult the style guidelines in Appendix B. This is especially important if you are entering your beer in a homebrew competition. If that is not your goal, decide what kind of body and alcohol content you want the beer to have, and choose an appropriate original gravity. The best way is to compare gravities for similar beers.

To determine the amount of grain needed to achieve the target gravity, apply the following formula: (Last 2 digits of OG) × gallons of beer × 1000/extraction rate = pounds of grain. If you do not know your extraction rate, 29 is a good estimate. For example, to make 10 gallons of beer with a starting gravity of 1.060, you need: 60 × 10/29 = 20.7 pounds of grain.

You can determine your extraction rate (or mash tun efficiency) by this same formula. You need to know the volume of the runnings collected. You can make yourself a quick dipstick and calibrate it with your kettle. You will also need to know the starting gravity. It is best to collect the sample after the kettle has begun its boil because the wort will then be properly mixed. Then you'll need to cool it down to 60°F and take a hydrometer reading. Remember that you will be collecting more wort than the final desired volume because of evaporation during the boil. This will also cause the original gravity to increase by several points. The formula to use is: Last 2 digits of specific gravity × gallons collected/pounds of grain used. Let's say we collected 12 gallons of runnings, and the gravity tested out to 1.052. Having used 20.7 pounds of grain, we determine our extraction rate to be: 52 × 12/20.7 = 30.14. This can be read as 1.03014 degrees of specific gravity per pound of grain used. Extraction rates will vary slightly from batch to batch, so take readings from several batches to determine what efficiency your system yields.

Drew believes a grain bill ideally should consist of at least three different grains. Pale malt will be the main ingredient, with other malts, like Munich, crystal, chocolate, and black, adding body and color to the beer. If you want to add alcohol without adding body, use honey or corn sugar, brown sugar, or molasses. These ingredients ferment out more fully, leaving very little residual sugars to contribute to body. Use these sparingly because they quickly make a beer appear thin. Other specialty malts, such as flaked barley, oats, and wheat, can also be used. These three aid the beer in foaming and head retention. Wheat ferments out more completely than barley and is a good choice if you require a low final gravity and a light color. Each of these components adds its own distinctive color, flavor, and aroma, which needs to be considered when determining the grain bill.

In selecting hops for your recipe, familiarize yourself with the distinctive characteristics and traditional uses of as many varieties as possible. Then balance and complement the flavors of your grains and other ingredients. Drew likes the citrusy notes of Chinook in fruit beers, and spicy Tettnanger provides a point of interest in crisp, straightforward lagers. The appropriate amount depends largely on the style, but generally the bittering hops balance the malt without overshadowing it. This, of course, is largely a question of taste, so consult guidelines and apply your own preferences.

When Drew designed recipes for his clients in Japan, he discovered that the Japanese palate doesn't appreciate bitterness. His Pale Ale, the hoppiest recipe he gave the Japanese, was designed with half the bitterness of what he considers "normal"—only 19 IBUs (International Bitterness Units). "In this case I wasn't making the beer to please myself. I needed to make it acceptable to the customers."

Drew boils his wort for 30 minutes before adding the hops, to get a good protein break. This is the time to peer into the kettle and see the warping star field. He then boils the first hop addition for 1 hour. "To extract maximum bitterness from the hops, you need to boil them for at least 45 minutes," he explains. Several late additions of hops add character and depth to Drew's beers. He uses as many as three different varieties in the last 30 minutes, added at three intervals—perhaps at the last 20-, last 10-, and last-minute marks. Because they do not boil for a long time, they contribute mostly flavor and aroma characteristics; the bitterness they contribute is negligible.

Dry hopping contributes the top note of aroma to beer without adding any bitterness. How much you use, and whether you use hops at all, is pretty much a matter of taste, but Drew recommends starting with a small amount the first time you dry-hop and adjusting from there. "Dry hopping with Chinook and Cascade will give you that distinctive Northwest taste," Drew says.

The most important consideration concerning yeast selection is choosing the right yeast for the recipe you are brewing. If you are making a pale ale, choosing a Belgian yeast strain or a lager yeast will leave you extremely disappointed. Liquid yeast always makes a better brew than dried yeast, assuming you grow it up properly. Procuring a good, healthy, clean strain will improve your beers greatly. "Befriend your local brewer," Drew advises. "Most brewers, especially those on the West Coast, are more than happy to give a local homebrewer a cup of yeast. Bringing along a six-pack of your own homebrew will serve as a nice payment," says Drew.

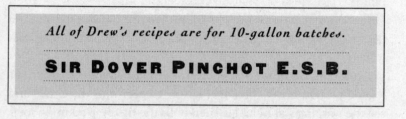

**All of Drew's recipes are for 10-gallon batches.**

## SIR DOVER PINCHOT E.S.B.

15 POUNDS MARIS OTTER PALE 2-ROW MALT
5 POUNDS BELGIAN CARA-PILS MALT
2 POUNDS CRYSTAL MALT (40L)
1 POUND DARK BROWN SUGAR
1 1/3 OUNCES NUGGET HOPS, PELLETS, 16.6% ALPHA
1 1/3 OUNCES FUGGLES HOPS, WHOLE FLOWERS, 5.0% ALPHA
1 1/3 OUNCES FUGGLES HOPS, WHOLE FLOWERS, 5.0% ALPHA
WYEAST LONDON ALE YEAST

OG: 1.060 • FG: 1.016

**M**ash grains at 155°F for 60 minutes. Boil for 90 minutes, adding 1 1/3 ounces Nugget hops after 30 minutes, 1 1/3 ounces Fuggles hops after 70 minutes, and 1 1/3 ounces Fuggles hops for the last minute. Cool wort and pitch yeast. Ferment for 1 week. Transfer to a secondary fermenter. Ferment for 3 days. Cool to 40°F and condition for an additional 4 days. Bottle or keg. Age 5 to 7 days before serving.

# FORGOTTEN WATERS
# PORTER

17 POUNDS ENGLISH 2-ROW MALT

2 POUNDS CRYSTAL MALT (60L)

3/4 POUND BELGIAN CHOCOLATE MALT

1/2 POUND ROAST BARLEY

1 1/3 OUNCES GALENA HOPS, WHOLE FLOWERS, 12.8% ALPHA

1 3/4 OUNCES CASCADE HOPS, WHOLE FLOWERS, 3.7% ALPHA

1 1/3 OUNCES TETTNANGER HOPS, WHOLE FLOWERS,
4.1% ALPHA

LIQUID FULLER'S STRAIN

OG: 1.056 • FG: 1.014

Mash grains at 149°F for 60 minutes. Boil for 90 minutes, adding Galena hops after 30 minutes, Cascade hops after 60 minutes, and Tettnanger hops for the last 10 minutes. Cool wort and pitch yeast. Ferment for 1 week. Transfer to a secondary fermenter. Ferment for 3 days. Cool to 40°F, and condition for an additional 4 days. Bottle or keg. Age 5 to 7 days before serving.

# BELGIAN SAISON

This was a summer seasonal beer produced by Pyramid Ales from May through August 1996, based on this original recipe.

14 POUNDS AMERICAN 2-ROW PALE MALT

6 POUNDS BELGIAN PILSNER MALT

3/4 POUND FLAKED BARLEY

1/2 POUND CARA VIENNA MALT

3 OUNCES SAAZ HOPS, PELLETS, 5.3% ALPHA

3/4 OUNCE TETTNANGER HOPS, WHOLE FLOWERS, 4.1% ALPHA

3/4 OUNCE SAAZ HOPS, PELLETS, 5.3% ALPHA

3/4 OUNCE SAAZ HOPS

WYEAST ABBEY ALE YEAST (CHIMAY)

OG: 1.054 • TG: 1.010

Mash grains at 152°F for 60 minutes. Boil for 90 minutes, adding 3 ounces Saaz hops after 30 minutes. Add 3/4 ounce Tettnanger hops after 70 minutes and the other 3/4 ounce Tettnanger hops and 3/4 ounce Saaz hops for the last 5 minutes. Cool wort and pitch yeast. Ferment for 3 days. Add 3/4 ounce Saaz hops, and ferment an additional 4 days. Transfer to a secondary fermenter. Ferment for 3 days. Cool to 40°F and condition for an additional 4 days. Bottle or keg. Age 5 to 7 days before serving.

# 5TH SYMPHONY ALE OR
# BA NAN NAN NA...

19 1/2 POUNDS AMERICAN 6-ROW PALE MALT
2 POUNDS CRYSTAL MALT (40L)
2 OUNCES CHINOOK HOPS, WHOLE FLOWERS, 12.1% ALPHA
1/2 OUNCE TETTNANGER HOPS, WHOLE FLOWERS, 4.1% ALPHA
1 1/3 OUNCES TETTNANGER HOPS, WHOLE FLOWERS, 4.1% ALPHA
WYEAST LONDON ALE YEAST*

10 RIPE BANANAS

OG: 1.052 • TG: 1.008

Mash grains at 149°F for 60 minutes. Boil for 90 minutes, adding Chinook hops after 30 minutes, 1/2 ounce Tettnanger hops after 70 minutes, and 1 1/3 ounces Tettnanger hops for the final 5 minutes. Cool wort and pitch yeast. Ferment for 1 week.

Mash 10 ripe bananas in a food processor. Pasteurize them in 180°F water for 10 minutes. Allow the mixture to cool to 100°F. Transfer the beer to a secondary fermenter, and add the banana mixture. Ferment for 3 days. Cool to 40°F, and condition an additional 4 days. Bottle or keg.

**NOTE:** *When racking off the secondary fermenter, it is necessary to "punch" through the floating banana layer and watch carefully for any rogue banana pieces that might clog your racking cane.*

Age 5 to 7 days before serving.

* Brewer's Note: "Any London ale strain will do. I tried using Chimay strain because I thought the banana esters would add to the flavor. The London ale batch was better by far. The trick here is to experiment. This beer can be made many different ways."

# 4.

## BILL OWENS

### Buffalo Bill's Brewery

*"I was not a particularly good homebrewer.
Sometimes I got it right. Sometimes I didn't."*

**W**hen Buffalo Bill Owens began homebrewing, John Kennedy was president, Mickey Mantle played for the New York Yankees, and the Beatles were still a club band. Bill refined and perfected the camping cooler/mash tun and wrote *How to Build a Small Brewery*. In 1983, he opened the first brewpub in California: Buffalo Bill's Brewery in Hayward, California. And he pioneered brewing journalism when he founded *The American Brewer* magazine. Buffalo Bill is a true beer pioneer.

In 1963, homebrewing was a long way from becoming legalized, and raw materials were hard to come by. "You could go into a market and buy premier malt," recalls Bill. "But there was a piece of paper attached to it that said, 'Do not add 5 gallons of water. Do not boil. Do not cool. Do not add yeast.'"

While teaching a photography course at the University of California at San Francisco, he met Guy Pawson, an Englishman teaching a homebrewing course down the hall. It was from Guy that Bill learned the basics of mashing. "He actually mashed into a zinc camping cooler, and put it in the oven overnight," Bill says. A course with a man named Michael Lewis led Bill to understand the simplicity of single-infusion mashing. With the difficulties of decoction and lautering rendered unnecessary, Bill incorporated a design for wort collection that he had seen at Budweiser. He put a slotted copper tube in the bottom of an insulated cooler, paving the way for the false bottoms commonly available today. Bill feels the most important aspect of the brewing process is in the mash. "To me, the whole heart is starch conversion. Everything else can be diddled with."

Bill's approach to the rest of the brewing process is quite straightforward, if not somewhat cavalier. Selection of raw materials should be based on availability. "I defy anyone to tell the difference between the same beer made with two-row and six-row malt in a blind taste test." To boost alcohol content, Bill often adds a few pounds of cane sugar to the boiling wort.

Bill doesn't really believe that late hop additions add flavor or aroma to the beer. Though he does use them now ("just for the hell of it"), he never employed finishing hops in his early days. Bill claims, "This stuff about late additions is a lot of baloney, because all of the aromatics are gone as soon as it hits and steams." That said, Bill feels the best way to infuse hop aroma into your beer is to use a hop-back. (See Appendix A for an easy way for homebrewers to capture hop aroma: the hop tea chamber.)

As for the common grudge that homebrewers harbor against dry yeast, Bill proclaims, "Malarkey." Plan ahead and rehydrate the yeast with 100°F water, and then allow the solution to cool to 70°F before pitching so as not to shock the yeast. When reusing yeast, Bill recalls his early homebrewing experience with amusement: "After two or three generations, the yeast would become deficient in zinc. I would keep the yeast in a galvanized mop bucket, and galvanization is zinc. I have a mop bucket I've saved, and all the galvinization has been eaten off by hundreds and hundreds of generations of yeast." Today yeast nutrients are available to add to the yeast.

Bill has little fear of contamination during fermentation and uses open vessels at the brewpub and at home. "There are a lot of advantages to open fermentation. It makes it easier to collect yeast, and there's something about the romance of watching the fermentation. I promise you, no airborne germ is gonna fly in there." What about simply adding a blow-off hose? Bill responds, "It's just something else to clean. Use a piece of tin foil."

Bill Owens is probably best known for the first commercially produced pumpkin ale in America. After brewing his first one using pumpkin in the mash, Bill discovered that the wort contained virtually no unique flavor—or no flavors that people would recognize as pumpkin. He soon realized that the key was in the spices. Bill adds his spice combination at packaging by making a spice tea, placing the spices in a coffee filter and running hot water through them, then adding this mixture to the beer before packaging. Bill believes this procedure works best for all untraditional flavorings or spices. "I want to keep the chemistry of beer as pure as I can. I don't want to be putting other crap in there that I can't control. If I do it in the bright beer tank, I can control it," explains Bill.

One last simple tip that Bill has for improving brewing skills is to choose one beer and brew it over and over so you understand what's going on. "Don't go brewing a stout, and then an amber, and then a pilsner when you're starting out. Learn to brew."

# PUMPKIN ALE

18 POUNDS PALE 2-ROW MALT

6 POUNDS CRYSTAL MALT (80L)

4 OUNCES CASCADE HOPS

AMERICAN ALE YEAST

4 POUNDS PUMPKIN (FRESH, NOT CANNED)

1 TABLESPOON PUMPKIN PIE SPICE

3/4 POUND CORN SUGAR (WHEN NOT FORCE CARBONATING)

OG: 1.048 • FG: 1.012

Bake the pumpkin at 375° for 1 hour. At the same time, mash grains for 60 minutes at 152°F. Cool the pumpkin; then cut it into one-inch cubes and add to the mash. Sparge and collect wort. Boil for 90 minutes, adding the Cascade hops 10 minutes after the boil begins. Cool wort and pitch yeast. Ferment at 70°F for 3 days. Cool to 38°F and ferment an additional 4 to 6 days. On the day you're going to bottle or keg, bring 2 cups of water to a boil. Place the pumpkin pie spice in a coffee filter and run the water through to make a spice tea. Add the spice tea to the beer prior to bottling or kegging. Age 7 to 10 days before serving.

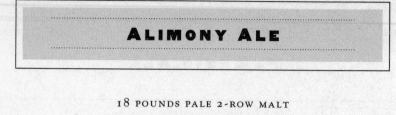

# ALIMONY ALE

18 POUNDS PALE 2-ROW MALT

2 POUNDS CRYSTAL MALT (120L)

8 OUNCES CASCADE HOPS

1 TEASPOON IRISH MOSS

AMERICAN ALE YEAST

OG: 1.046 • FG: 1.010

Mash grains for 60 to 90 minutes at 155°F. Sparge and collect wort. Boil for 90 minutes, adding all Cascade hops after 30 minutes and the Irish moss during the final 5 minutes. Cool wort and pitch yeast. Ferment at 70°F for 3 days. Cool to 38°F, and ferment an additional 4 to 6 days. Bottle or keg. Age 7 to 10 days before serving.

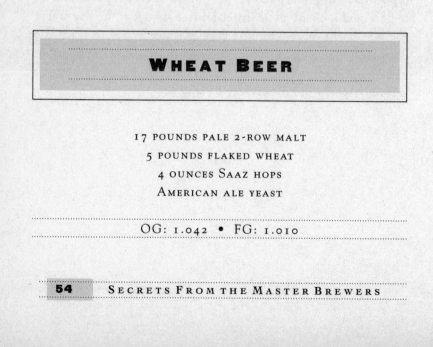

# WHEAT BEER

17 POUNDS PALE 2-ROW MALT

5 POUNDS FLAKED WHEAT

4 OUNCES SAAZ HOPS

AMERICAN ALE YEAST

OG: 1.042 • FG: 1.010

Mash grains for 60 minutes at 155°F. Sparge and collect wort. Boil for 90 minutes, adding the Saaz hops after 30 minutes. Cool wort and pitch yeast. Ferment at 70°F for 3 days. Cool to 38°F, and ferment an additional 4 to 6 days. Bottle or keg. Age 7 to 10 days before serving.

## IMPERIAL STOUT

20 POUNDS PALE 2-ROW MALT

3 POUNDS CRYSTAL MALT (120 L)

2 POUNDS BLACK PATENT MALT

2 POUNDS ROASTED BARLEY

10 OUNCES FUGGLES HOPS

AMERICAN ALE YEAST

2 POUNDS CANE SUGAR (OPTIONAL;
ADD TO THE BOIL FOR EXTRA STRENGTH)

OG: 1.072 • FG: 1.020

Mash grains for 60 minutes at 155°F. Sparge and collect wort. Boil for 90 minutes, adding the Fuggles hops after 30 minutes. Cool wort and pitch yeast. Ferment at 70°F for 3 days. Cool to 38°F, and ferment an additional 4 to 6 days. Bottle or keg. Age 7 to 10 days before serving.

# 5.

## DICK CANTWELL

### *Elysian Brewing Company*

*"I'm always tempted to throw a little German into a lot of my beers" (regarding hops, not Germans under 5 foot 1).*

In the eight years since Dick Cantwell began brewing as a professional, he has pioneered the beers at two new brewpubs, worked at a nationally renowned brewery, and assumed the head brewer role at a brewpub that had already garnered 11 Great American Beer Festival medals. He has learned a lot over the years.

When Dick relocated from Boston to Seattle, he was already an avid homebrewer and saw Seattle's burgeoning beer scene as an opportunity to make brewing his career. Armed with his homebrew portfolio, a mixed six-pack, he secured a job as head brewer at the soon-to-open Duwamps Cafe. Shortly before Duwamps closed in 1991, he had moved on to work under Fal Allen at Pike Place Brewery. In 1994, Dick was given the opportunity to hit the big time, as head brewer at the award-winning Big Time Brewing Company. He is currently head brewer at, and co-owner of, Elysian Brewing Company. Throughout the years, Dick has refined many aspects of the brewing process, from recipe formulation to brewing techniques. He passed along some tips and innovations that can be applied to homebrewing.

When it comes to grains, Dick has worked with a wide variety. "At Pike Place, we used Maris Otter, which I love. At Big Time, I experimented with German lager malts, which were not very effective without decoction." At Elysian, Dick uses American pale two-row malt as his base malt because it is versatile enough to use in both ales and lagers. When adding specialty grains, he uses crystal sparingly to avoid what he describes as "sticky sweetness." He prefers a drier finish and suggests, as a substitute, a small amount of roasted barley to attain the desired color. In pale lagers, Munich malt and dextrine malts, such as Carastan or Cara-Pils, are added in a two-to-one ratio to contribute some thickness to the lager's body. The quantity of grain is then scaled up or down depending on the style. "The Dortmunder is very similar to the maibock recipe, but those two grains have been scaled down to make it a somewhat drier beer," explains Dick.

When making German-style lagers, the challenge is finding a good German hop to provide adequate bitterness. Noble hops such as Hallertauer, Tettnanger, and Saaz are usually low in alpha acid. "Right now, I'm totally in love with the German Northern Brewer hops. Not only is the alpha higher, but it has a wonderful aroma. I've even started finishing my ale and porter with it," says Dick.

There's little point in blending hops in the boil, according to Dick, but the finish is another matter. "Most commonly I have a couple of hop varieties in the finish. I really like Styrian Goldings in the finish of my lagers." He uses Styrian Goldings in many of his ales as well to complement Cascade or Chinook. In some of the more Northwest styles, he'll add a blend of Centennial and Cascade or some other combination to add a spicy touch to the citrus.

Although Dick is limited by time and equipment to single-temperature or step-infusion mashing, he's an avid proponent of decoction for all lager beers. "Decoction is a pain in the ass, but it's always very rewarding. As a homebrewer, I always double-decocted all of my lagers."

Without decoction equipment, Dick can still manipulate his results by adjusting mash temperature. Higher mash temperatures activate the alpha-amylase enzymes, which leave less-fermentable sugars for higher body. Lower mash temperatures result in a thinner, drier beer.

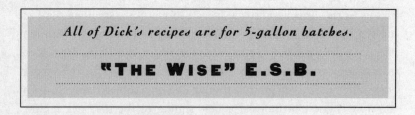

*All of Dick's recipes are for 5-gallon batches.*

## "THE WISE" E.S.B.

9 POUNDS PALE 2-ROW MALT

1 POUND CRYSTAL MALT (80L)

1 POUND MUNICH MALT

1/4 POUND CRYSTAL MALT (120L)

3/4 OUNCE CHINOOK HOPS

3/4 OUNCE CASCADE HOPS

3/4 OUNCE CENTENNIAL HOPS

3/4 OUNCE CASCADE HOPS

3/4 OUNCE CENTENNIAL HOPS

ALE YEAST

Mash grains for 60 to 90 minutes at 152–155°F. Sparge and collect wort. Bring wort to a boil, and add 3/4 ounce Chinook hops. Boil for 60 minutes, adding 3/4 ounce Cascade and 3/4 ounce Centennial hops for the final 2 minutes of the boil. Turn off the heat, add 3/4 ounce Cascade and 3/4 ounce Centennial hops, and let steep for 10 minutes. Cool wort and pitch yeast. Ferment for 4 to 6 days. Transfer to a secondary fermenter, and condition an additional 5 to 7 days. Bottle or keg. Age 7 to 10 days before serving.

# PERSEUS PORTER

9 POUNDS 2-ROW PALE MALT

1/2 POUND CRYSTAL MALT (80L)

1 POUND MUNICH MALT

6 OUNCES CHOCOLATE MALT

6 OUNCES BLACK MALT

1/2 OUNCE CENTENNIAL HOPS

1 OUNCE GERMAN NORTHERN BREWER HOPS

ALE YEAST

Mash grains for 60 to 90 minutes at 152–155°F. Sparge and collect wort. Bring wort to a boil, and add Centennial hops. Boil for 60 minutes, adding German Northern Brewer hops for the final 2 minutes of the boil. Cool wort and pitch yeast. Ferment for 4 to 6 days. Transfer to a secondary fermenter, and condition an additional 5 to 7 days. Bottle or keg. Age 7 to 10 days before serving.

# LOKI LAGER

## Dortmunder Style

9 POUNDS 2-ROW PALE MALT

1 POUND MUNICH MALT

1/2 POUND PALE CARAMALT

1 OUNCE GERMAN NORTHERN BREWER HOPS

3/4 OUNCE STYRIAN GOLDINGS HOPS

3/4 OUNCE STYRIAN GOLDINGS HOPS

LAGER YEAST

Mash grains for 60 to 90 minutes at 152–155°F. Sparge and collect wort. Bring wort to a boil, and add German Northern Brewer hops. Boil for 60 minutes, adding 3/4 ounce Styrian Goldings hops for the final 2 minutes of the boil. Turn off the heat, add 3/4 ounce Styrian Goldings hops. Let steep for 10 minutes. Cool wort and pitch yeast. Ferment for 7 to 10 days at 45°F. Transfer to a secondary fermenter, and condition at 45°F for an additional 3 to 4 weeks. Bottle or keg. Age 7 to 10 days before serving.

# PANDORA'S WILD FLING

## Wild Rice Bock

11 1/4 POUNDS 2-ROW PALE MALT

1 POUND MUNICH MALT

3/4 POUND DARK CARAMALT (45L)

2 POUNDS WHOLE WILD RICE

1 1/4 OUNCES GERMAN NORTHERN BREWER HOPS

1/2 OUNCE STYRIAN GOLDINGS HOPS

3/4 OUNCE STYRIAN GOLDINGS HOPS

LAGER YEAST

Cook the rice according to the package directions. Add to the top of mash at mash-in. Mash grains for 60 to 90 minutes at 152–155°F. Sparge and collect wort. Bring wort to a boil, and add German Northern Brewer hops. Boil for 60 minutes, adding 1/2 ounce Styrian Goldings hops for the final 2 minutes of the boil. Turn off the heat, and add 3/4 ounce Styrian Goldings hops. Let steep for 10 minutes. Cool wort and pitch yeast. Ferment for 7 to 10 days at 45°F. Transfer to a secondary fermenter, and condition an additional 4 to 6 weeks at 43°F. Bottle or keg. Age 10 to 14 days before serving.

# EVACUTINUS

## Dark Weizenbock

**T**his beer was first brewed at Elysian's small brewery located at Gameworks in Seattle in an effort to replicate Schneider's Aventinus. In the course of the brew, the steam from the kettle triggered the fire alarm system, forcing the evacuation of the entire Gameworks facility (the Steven Spielberg–owned facility), as well as 16 movie theaters in the multiplex next door. Hence the name. Oh, the power of beer.

7 POUNDS 2-ROW PALE MALT

9 1/4 POUNDS WHEAT MALT

1/2 POUND CRYSTAL MALT (80L)

1 1/4 POUNDS MUNICH MALT

3/4 POUND CARAMALT (11L)

1/2 POUND CARAFA OR OTHER DARK CRYSTAL MALT

1 1/4 OUNCES GERMAN NORTHERN BREWER HOPS

2 1/4 OUNCES GERMAN NORTHERN BREWER HOPS

BELGIAN TRAPPIST YEAST

**M**ash grains for 60 to 90 minutes at 152–155°F. Sparge and collect wort. Bring wort to a boil, and add 1 1/4 ounces German Northern Brewer hops. Boil for 60 minutes. Turn off heat, and add 2 1/4 ounces German Northern Brewer hops. Let steep for 10 minutes. Cool wort and pitch yeast. Ferment for 5 to 7 days. Transfer to a secondary fermenter, and condition an additional 7 to 10 days. Bottle or keg. Age 14 to 21 days before serving.

# 6.

## LUCA EVANS AND NICK HANKIN

### *The Highlander Brewery*

*"If you keg beer, you stop the life of the beer and create boundaries. If you cask-condition beer, it allows the yeast to keep developing, mutating, and changing the beer into so many levels that theoretically you have an infinite number of flavor levels. It is basically chaos theory!"*
*(Nick Hankin)*

Nick Hankin was born in Ireland and started homebrewing as a teenager. After attending Simon's Rock of Bard College, where he met Luca Evans, Nick set out for Europe, where he traveled for two years sampling beers and learning from master brewers. In 1994, he apprenticed under Vic Norton, Cellarman of the Year for 12 years in a row for the Greenalls pub chain in England at the Glass Cutter Arms. Upon completing his training, he returned to America, to join his brothers and Luca Evans in a brewpub venture in New York City.

Luca Evans joined Nick in New York to serve as head brewer at the Highlander Brewery and fulfill their lifelong dream of owning a brewpub together. Luca began his brewing career at the Shipyard Brewing Company in Portland, Maine, where he trained under renowned British brewmaster Alan Pugsley. He then moved on to assume the position of head brewer at Barley Creek Brewing in Tannersville, Pennsylvania.

The Highlander Brewery was founded as a Scottish ale brewery with a strong emphasis on cask-conditioned ales. Utilizing excess brewing capacity at Middle Ages Brewing Company in Syracuse, New York, Luca and Nick designed and brewed their beers for dispense at their New York City location. Although the pub no longer exists, the Highlander Brewery continues to brew beer for distribution in the New York City area. In its first year of business, the Highlander became the largest producer of cask-conditioned beers in America. Their 80/Shilling Brown garnered the Award of Excellence at the 1996 Real Ale Festival in Chicago, finishing behind Sir Anthony Fuller's Cask Conditioned ESB and Marsden's Old Roger, but beating out two other Fuller's, three other Marsden's, and every American entry. Michael Jackson has called their 60 Shilling Dark Mild "a perfect example of the style." In addition to maintaining the Highlander brands, Nick and Luca have endeavored to educate the market through their Real Ale Consulting business, which provides tavern owners with the proper techniques for handling and serving "living beer."

## BREWING CASK-CONDITIONED BEERS

Cask conditioning is the traditional method of packaging beer after fermentation for aging and serving. Prior to the development of filtration and forced carbonation, all beer was essentially cask- (or bottle-) conditioned. Cask-conditioned ales continue to be the preferred style in the United Kingdom, where they are known as "real ales," so it is most appropriate for styles originating there. It differs from bottle conditioning in that it allows the entire batch of beer to condition as a whole, resulting in a rounder, mellower, more consistent flavor.

The key to developing a recipe destined for the cask is to use authentic British ingredients. Proper English-style two-row malts, such as Maris Otter and Pipkin, result in a full, round malt flavor. "Malts like mild malt, pale malt, and Scottish malt have all been developed over centuries for particular styles," explains Luca. "It makes sense to use them for the appropriate style."

Since cask-conditioned ales cannot be filtered, preventing the development of haze is a primary concern in recipe formulation. Sugar adjuncts are widely used in real ales because they contribute fermentables without adding proteins that may result in haze. Brewer's sugar, brown sugar, molasses, and treacle are common kettle additions.

British hops like East Kent Goldings and Fuggles are much less assertive than the varieties available in America and from Germany. It is possible to use other hops, but Nick recommends cellaring the cask longer to allow the more distinctive hops to meld with the malts.

A hearty English ale yeast is essential—one that is highly attenuating and highly flocculant. Fermentation schedule and cellaring technique are dictated by the characteristics of the particular strain. Less attenuative strains may require the addition of priming sugar to the cask. Less flocculant yeast strains require the addition of finings in order to drop out of the beer before serving, or "drop bright."

Water treatment is a crucial factor in the success of all stages of brewing British ales, from the mash through fermentation. "You can buy malt, hops, and yeast for a particular style, but you can't do that with water," offers Nick. Soft water naturally lends itself to malty styles of ales. If you are brewing a Burton-style pale ale or an India pale ale, it is necessary to add gypsum. For all styles, mash water should have a pH between 4.0 and 5.0 for optimal enzyme activity. Gypsum added during the mash helps keep the pH from skyrocketing after the enzymes begin their work in the mash tun.

For the Highlander's Scottish ales, Nick and Luca replicated the hardness, pH, gypsum (calcium sulfate), magnesium sulfate, sodium, and chlorine levels of Edinborough water. To obtain a similar authentic flavor in a regional style, obtain a water profile from your local water provider. Then consult the chart in the back of

Greg Noonan's *The New Brewing Lager Beer* to determine the hardness, pH, and mineral salt levels that you are seeking.

Brewing a cask-conditioned ale differs only slightly from the process for bottled beer. Again, the clarity of the finished product is an important focus. The use of kettle finings, such as Irish moss, and a good, rolling boil are essential for a good hot break. The removal of proteins in the kettle means that less fining will be necessary in later stages—a desirable outcome, because excessive finings affect the flavor of the beer.

Open fermentation is the traditional British technique for real ales. Few homebrewers are comfortable with open vessels due to the increased risk of contamination, and closed fermentation will suffice. Open fermentation offers the advantage of stripping yeast from the top. If it is not stripped, the yeast will settle down through the beer, increasing the amount in suspension. When using closed fermentation, rack the beer off of the flocculated yeast when the krausen stops flowing out of the blow-off hose.

Fermentation of real ales requires careful monitoring, with precise timing depending on the particular yeast strain, recipe, and fermentation conditions. Primary fermentation should be maintained at 68–70°F and typically takes 2 to 4 days. When the gravity is 2 to 3 points above the desired final gravity, strip off the yeast (or rack the beer) and chill to 40–45°F. This cold-conditioning stops fermentation and removes more yeast from suspension.

Directions for installing a sampling cock on a plastic fermenter are found in Appendix A. A sample cock will enable you to sample and monitor your beer without further risk of contamination. Be sure to take samples often as your beer nears the desired gravity, or you might miss your mark.

### CELLARING

When making a cask-conditioned beer, cellaring is as important as brewing. During cellaring, the beer will complete its final 2 to 3 degrees of fermentation, maintaining the carbon dioxide in suspension. The beer is fined to facilitate the final clarification. Priming sugar and hops may also be added at this time, if necessary or desired. The beer will be allowed to condition, then will be vented and served. Real ales deteriorate very quickly once they are vented, and should be consumed within 2 to 3 days.

The cellaring process begins by transfering the beer into its cask (see Appendix A for modification of a Cornelius keg for cask conditioning) when it has completed all but the final 2 to 3 points of fermentation. Two fining agents are added to the cask at this point. Isinglass is used to aid in the settling of yeast cells. Isinglass is collagen derived from the swim bladders of sturgeon fish. Its amino acids are broken down into long strands, with a positive molecular charge able to flocculate the negatively charged yeast cells and pull them to the bottom of the vessel. Alginex aids in the settling of proteins. It is produced from carageenan and has a negative charge so it can attract and drop out positively charged proteins. It works in basically the same way as carageenan kettle finings (Irish moss).

Priming sugars may also be added to the cask at this stage. If your beer has passed the desired target gravity (2 to 3 points above full attenuation), it is necessary to add priming sugars for adequate carbonation. If the beer has fully attenuated, add 3/4 cup of corn sugar per 5 gallons. If it is 1 degree above final gravity, add 1/2 cup. If it is between 1 1/2 and 2 points above, add 1/4 cup. Remember that it is better to add extra sugars than to have too little; as Nick says, "It's easy to condition down. It's much harder to condition up."

Many real ales benefit from the addition of dry hops to the cask. If you so desire, add a handful of fresh hops—or 1/2 to 3/4 ounce per 5 gallons. Fresh hop flowers are preferable, but plugs will suffice. Avoid pellets. To prevent clogging while pouring, place the hops in a hop bag. In addition to adding aroma, hops aid in preservation during the conditioning process.

If you're able to, lay the cask on its side at this point, with the serving nozzle at the bottom. Bring the cask to 52–54°F. The cask will be maintained at this temperature throughout cellaring and serving. Fluctuations in temperature may result in off-flavors. The amount of time to condition the beer depends on the beer's original gravity. Beers like milds, with original gravities between 1.031 and 1.034, should be conditioned for 7 days. Beers like bitters and ESBs, with original gravities between 1.034 and 1.042, require 2 to 2 1/2 weeks. Pale ales, brown ales, and Scottish ales, with original gravities between 1.045 to 1.055, require 3 to 4 weeks. Beers with original gravities above 1.060 require 4 to 6 weeks. Really big beers like barleywines and old ales should condition for a minimum of 6 months. Stouts, while relatively low in gravity, are particularly acidic and benefit from a couple of extra weeks of conditioning. Remember that these are guidelines. Your own brew may take longer. Even a particular recipe may not conform to a regular conditioning schedule because each batch reacts differently. Check the carbonation of your beer by swishing it around in your mouth. You should feel the beer's "bursting bubbles." If you don't, seal the cask back up, and allow the beer to condition further.

### SERVING

It is traditional to gravity-pour cask-conditioned beers. If you were unable to lay your cask on its side during conditioning, do so now, and allow it to settle for 12 hours. Attach the air-in hose to the cask. Don't be surprised if you get a "beer shower" as the excess pressure is released from the cask.

Allow the cask to sit for 1 1/2 hours. Then attach the dispense hose and pour. If the beer will be completely consumed within 12 hours, you can attach an air pump to the air-in hose and push the beer. Longer exposure to air will eliminate the protective blanket of carbon dioxide and push air into the beer. Do *not* attach a carbon dioxide tank and push the beer with gas, because it will no longer be considered real ale. Isn't that why you've gone to all this trouble in the first place?

# ROWDY RODDY PIPER
# 90/SHILLING HEAVY ALE

12 POUNDS PALE 2-ROW BRITISH MALT

1 POUND TORREFIED WHEAT

3/4 POUND CRYSTAL MALT (60L)

1/4 POUND CARAMEL MALT

1 OUNCE ROASTED BARLEY

1 1/2 OUNCES FUGGLES HOPS

1/2 OUNCE FUGGLES HOPS

1 OUNCE KENT GOLDINGS HOPS

2 TEASPOONS IRISH MOSS

WYEAST 1728 SCOTTISH ALE YEAST

OG: 1.075

Mash grains at 152°F for 60 minutes. Sparge and collect wort. Bring wort to a boil, and add 1 1/2 ounces Fuggles hops. Boil for 90 minutes. Add 1/2 ounce Fuggles hops, Kent Goldings hops, and Irish moss for the final 5 minutes. Cool wort and pitch yeast. Follow the fermentation and kegging schedule already set out in this chapter.

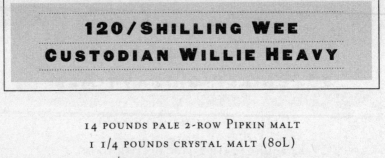

## 120/SHILLING WEE
## CUSTODIAN WILLIE HEAVY

14 POUNDS PALE 2-ROW PIPKIN MALT

1 1/4 POUNDS CRYSTAL MALT (80L)

1 1/4 POUNDS TORREFIED WHEAT

3/4 POUND CARAMEL MALT

1/4 POUND CHOCOLATE MALT

1/8 POUND ROASTED BARLEY

2 OUNCES FUGGLES HOPS

1 1/4 OUNCES FUGGLES HOPS

WYEAST 1728 SCOTTISH ALE YEAST

OG: 1.095

Mash grains at 152°F for 60 minutes. Sparge and collect wort. Bring wort to a boil, and add 2 ounces Fuggles hops. Boil for 90 minutes, adding 1 1/4 ounces Fuggles hops and the Irish moss for the final 5 minutes. Cool wort and pitch yeast. Follow the fermentation and kegging schedule already set out in this chapter.

# NORTON'S NECTAR

13 POUNDS PALE 2-ROW MARIS OTTER MALT
3/4 POUNDS CRYSTAL MALT (60L)
3/4 POUND TORREFIED WHEAT
3/4 POUND CARAMEL MALT
2 OUNCES FUGGLES HOPS
1 1/2 OUNCES EAST KENT GOLDINGS HOPS
2 TEASPOONS IRISH MOSS
WYEAST 1728 SCOTTISH ALE YEAST

OG: 1.083

Mash grains at 152°F for 60 minutes. Sparge and collect wort. Bring wort to a boil, and add Fuggles hops. Boil for 90 minutes, adding the East Kent Golding hops and Irish moss for the final 5 minutes. Cool wort and pitch yeast. Follow the fermentation and kegging schedule already set out in this chapter.

# 60/SHILLING DARK MILD

6 POUNDS PALE 2-ROW MARIS OTTER MALT

1/2 POUND CRYSTAL MALT (80L)

1/2 POUND TORREFIED WHEAT

1/2 POUND CARAMEL MALT

1/2 POUND CHOCOLATE MALT

3/4 OUNCE FUGGLES HOPS

3/4 OUNCE EAST KENT GOLDINGS HOPS

1 OUNCE EAST KENT GOLDINGS HOPS

1 1/4 OUNCES FUGGLES HOPS

1 TEASPOON IRISH MOSS

WYEAST 1728 SCOTTISH ALE YEAST

OG: 1.033

Mash grains at 152°F for 60 minutes. Sparge and collect wort. Bring wort to a boil, and add 3/4 ounce Fuggles hops and 3/4 ounce East Kent Goldings hops. Boil for 90 minutes, adding 1 ounce East Kent Goldings hops, 1 1/4 ounces Fuggles hops, and Irish moss for the final 5 minutes. Cool wort and pitch yeast. Follow the fermentation and kegging schedule already set out in this chapter.

# 70/SHILLING ALE

6 POUNDS PALE 2-ROW BRITISH MALT

1/2 POUND CRYSTAL MALT (60L)

1/2 POUND TORREFIED WHEAT

1/4 POUND CARAMEL MALT

1/2 POUND LIGHT BROWN SUGAR

1 1/2 OUNCES KENT GOLDINGS HOPS

1 OUNCE FUGGLES HOPS

2 TEASPOONS IRISH MOSS

WYEAST 1728 SCOTTISH ALE YEAST

## OG: 1.043

Mash grains at 152°F for 60 minutes. Sparge and collect wort. Bring wort to a boil, and add Kent Goldings hops. Boil for 90 minutes, adding Fuggles hops and Irish moss for the final 5 minutes. Cool wort and pitch yeast. Follow the fermentation and kegging schedule already set out in this chapter.

# TONGAN DEATH GRIP
# BROWN ALE

8 1/2 POUNDS PALE 2-ROW MARIS OTTER MALT

1/2 POUND CRYSTAL MALT (80L)

1/2 POUND TORREFIED WHEAT

1/2 POUND CARAMEL MALT

1/2 POUND CHOCOLATE MALT

1 OUNCE FUGGLES HOPS

1 OUNCE EAST KENT GOLDINGS HOPS

1 OUNCE FUGGLES HOPS

3/4 OUNCE EAST KENT GOLDINGS HOPS

1 TEASPOON IRISH MOSS

WYEAST 1098 BRITISH ALE YEAST

## OG: 1.052

**M**ash grains at 152°F for 60 minutes. Sparge and collect wort. Bring wort to a boil, and add 1 ounce Fuggles hops and 1 ounce East Kent Goldings hops. Boil for 90 minutes, adding 1 ounce Fuggles hops, 3/4 ounce East Kent Goldings hops, and Irish moss for the final 5 minutes. Cool wort and pitch yeast. Follow the fermentation and kegging schedule already set out in this chapter.

# 7.

## DON GORTEMILLER

### *Pacific Coast Brewing Company*

*"There are quite a few all-grain brewers who
don't have as many medals as I do."*

**S**o you think that award-winning beers need to be brewed using all grain? Well, maybe you should talk to Don Gortemiller while he's wearing his nine Great American Beer Festival medals. Don brews award-winning extract-based beers at the Pacific Coast Brewing Company in Oakland, California. He has won medals for seven straight years—a record for a brewpub.

One of Don's college friends at the University of California at Berkeley (and now a partner at Pacific Coast) got Don started homebrewing with a homebrew kit as a Christmas present in 1975. "The first beer I made was a stout, which was fantastic, and the next few were pretty much complete disasters, but I was hooked," said Don. For the next 12 years, he pursued his hobby, winning several awards, including a bronze medal at the National Homebrew Competition, all the time making extract-based beers. In 1988 he decided to make his hobby his profession by opening Pacific Coast—and, yes, still brewing extract-based beers. "If it ain't broke, don't fix it," explains Don.

Not every homebrewer has the time, money, or space to move up to all grain, so we talked to Don about how extract brewers can make their beers as good as, or even better than, their all-grain relatives.

## EXTRACT BREWING

When homebrewers move up to all grain, they implement a lot of other changes in addition to starting with grain. They begin to use a full-wort boil, they add a wort chiller, some start to ferment in glass instead of plastic, and they make a number of other improvements and upgrades. "First-time grain brewers have this host of things that they've improved on, and then when the beer's better, they say, 'Oh, it was all in the grain.' But it's not. It's everything," explains Don.

The first thing an extract brewer should do is to buy an 8- to 10-gallon brewpot to enable them to perform a full-wort boil. "Throw away those 2-gallon pots," advises Don. Find a pot with a good, thick bottom. Try to avoid thin-bottomed pots or enameled pots. A full-wort boil helps to eliminate one of the major factors that contributes to the "extract flavor," which is caramelization of the wort. Going to a full-wort boil will also decrease the chance of infection, since you don't have to hope that the additional 4 gallons of cold water you're adding are sterile.

Possibly the most important improvement is hop utilization, which is directly related to the density of the wort. Hop calculations are usually based on fully diluted wort. In a concentrated boil, however, the hops will not produce the bitterness you calculated since the wort you're boiling is much denser and will react with the hops differently. The addition of a wort chiller, essential when going to a full-wort boil, will improve extract beers by reducing the chance of infection.

Switching to a glass fermenter from a plastic one is another simple change that extract brewers can make. Most homebrew kits come with a plastic bucket as a fermenter, but they scratch easily and wear out quickly. These scratches harbor bacteria, which could lead to infection. An investment of $15 to $20 for a glass fermenter will make a big difference.

The basis of extract beers is malt extract. Here are Don's guidelines for choosing an extract that will improve your beer. First, choose a locally produced extract, or as locally as possible, while avoiding imported extracts. "Because of the scale of economics, foreign extracts have to be more concentrated, which causes them to be darker and more caramelized," explains Don. Use the palest extract available, avoiding the amber or dark extracts. Extract producers don't provide a breakdown of the grain bill used to produce these darker extracts, which leaves you with a lot of guesswork in terms of which and how much specialty grains need to be added when making darker beers. "You can always make a beer darker, but you can't make it lighter," says Don. Avoid prehopped extracts because they contain elements that can't be removed. Also, hopped extract is probably the single biggest factor that contributes that signature "extract flavor."

Make sure that you don't pour all the extract into the pot and then begin stirring. Stir constantly while adding extract to the pot to prevent the extract from caramelizing (scorching) on the bottom.

Adding a blend of specialty grains will also make dramatic improvements in extract beers by contributing color, flavor, and aroma. When using specialty grains, steep them in 155°F water for 15 to 20 minutes, and then remove them. Do not add your grain to cold water and remove it as the water comes to a boil. As the water gets above 190°F (a boil is 212°F), tannins and astringencies will be drawn out of the grain, contributing unpleasant flavors to the beer.

Which specialty grains to use is a matter of taste and personal preference. Crystal, chocolate, and roasted barley all work very well. Don is a big fan of black malt flour, which contributes color but not the bitterness or aroma associated with black malts. Don't bother using fermentable grains like pale and Munich; without mashing, there is no diastatic power to convert the starches to usable sugars.

Simply steeping the grains in hot water is more than adequate. But if you have the ability, building a 1-gallon mash tun can be very useful (see Appendix A) by allowing you to use fermentable grains in a mini-mash. With this system, it is possible to perform a partial mash, utilizing fermentable grains for a portion of your grain bill and thus permitting a wider range of flavors, options, and styles.

Finally, don't let *anyone* tell you that because you don't make your beers from all grain that you're not a real homebrewer. If they do, tell them about Don and his medals from the Great American Beer Festival.

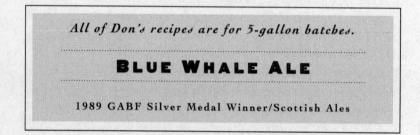

*All of Don's recipes are for 5-gallon batches.*

## BLUE WHALE ALE

**1989 GABF Silver Medal Winner/Scottish Ales**

8 POUNDS LIGHT MALT EXTRACT SYRUP

1 POUND CRYSTAL MALT (40L)

1 POUND CRYSTAL MALT (120L)

1.3 OUNCES NUGGET HOPS, 14.6% ALPHA

1.3 OUNCES CHINOOK HOPS, 11.3% ALPHA

0.8 OUNCE WILLAMETTE HOPS, 4.2% ALPHA

0.8 OUNCE CENTENNIAL HOPS, 10.9% ALPHA

0.5 OUNCE PERLE HOPS, 7.6% ALPHA

0.5 OUNCE CHINOOK HOPS, 11.3% ALPHA

1.5 OUNCES CENTENNIAL HOPS, 10.9% ALPHA

1.6 OUNCES OAK CHIPS (DRY HOP)

1 TEASPOON IRISH MOSS

YEAST NUTRIENT

ALE YEAST

Fill the brewpot with 6 gallons of water, and heat to 165°F. Add the crystal malt and steep for 20 minutes. Remove spent grain and bring wort to a boil. Turn off the heat and add malt extract syrup. Stir until completely dissolved and then return to heat. Add Nugget hops and 1.3 ounces Chinook hops. Boil for 90 minutes, adding Willamette, Perle, 0.8 ounces Centennial, and 0.5 ounces Perle hops for the final 20 minutes. Add Irish moss during the final 10 minutes. Cool wort and pitch yeast and yeast nutrient. Ferment 3 to 5 days and transfer to a secondary fermenter. Add 1.5 ounces Centennial hops and oak chips. Ferment an additional 5 to 7 days. Bottle or keg. Age 7 to 10 days before serving.

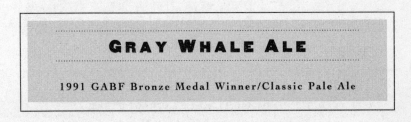

## GRAY WHALE ALE

**1991 GABF Bronze Medal Winner/Classic Pale Ale**

7 POUNDS LIGHT MALT EXTRACT SYRUP

1/2 POUND CRYSTAL MALT (20L)

.30 OUNCE NUGGET HOPS, 14.6% ALPHA

.50 OUNCE CHINOOK HOPS, 11.3% ALPHA

.20 OUNCE WILLAMETTE HOPS, 4.2% ALPHA

.20 OUNCE PERLE HOPS, 7.6% ALPHA

1 TEASPOON IRISH MOSS

YEAST NUTRIENT

ALE YEAST

**F**ill a brewpot with 6 gallons of water, and heat to 165°F. Add crystal malt, and steep for 20 minutes. Remove the spent grain, and bring wort to a boil. Turn off the heat and add the malt extract. Stir until completely dissolved, then return to the heat. Add Nugget hops and Chinook hops. Boil for 90 minutes, adding the Willamette and Perle hops for the final 20 minutes and the Irish moss during the final 10 minutes. Cool wort and pitch yeast and yeast nutrient. Ferment 3 to 5 days and transfer to a secondary fermenter. Ferment for an additional 5 to 7 days. Bottle or keg. Age 7 to 10 days before serving.

## KILLER WHALE STOUT

**1990 GABF Silver Medal Winner/Stout**
**1991 GABF Honorable Mention/Stout**

6.5 POUNDS LIGHT MALT EXTRACT SYRUP

.63 POUND CRYSTAL MALT (120L)

.50 POUND BLACK MALT FLOUR

.13 POUND CHOCOLATE MALT

.52 POUND ROASTED BARLEY

.60 OUNCE NUGGET HOPS, 14.6% ALPHA

1 OUNCE CHINOOK HOPS, 11.3% ALPHA

.70 OUNCE WILLAMETTE HOPS, 4.2% ALPHA

1 TEASPOON IRISH MOSS

YEAST NUTRIENT

ALE YEAST

**F**ill the brewpot with 6 gallons of water, and heat to 165°F. Add crystal malt, chocolate malt, and roasted barley. Steep for 20 minutes. Remove spent grain, and bring wort to a boil. Turn off the heat and add malt extract syrup and black malt flour. Stir until completely dissolved and then return to the heat. Add Nugget hops and Chinook hops. Boil for 90 minutes, adding Willamette hops for the final 20 minutes and Irish moss for the final 10 minutes. Cool wort and pitch yeast and yeast nutrient. Ferment 3 to 5 days, and transfer to a secondary fermenter. Ferment an additional 5 to 7 days. Bottle or keg. Age 7 to 10 days before serving.

## IMPERIAL STOUT

1992 GABF Silver Medal/Strong Ale
1993 GABF Silver Medal/Strong Ale

8.5 POUNDS LIGHT MALT EXTRACT SYRUP

.63 POUND CRYSTAL MALT (120L)

1 POUND BLACK MALT FLOUR

.50 POUND CHOCOLATE MALT

.75 POUND ROASTED BARLEY

1.5 POUNDS HONEY

.80 OUNCE NUGGET HOPS, 14.6% ALPHA

1 OUNCE CHINOOK HOPS, 11.3% ALPHA

.75 OUNCE CHINOOK HOPS, 11.3% ALPHA

1 TEASPOON IRISH MOSS

YEAST NUTRIENT

ALE YEAST

Fill the brewpot with 6 gallons of water, and heat to 165°F. Add crystal malt, chocolate malt, and roasted barley. Steep for 20 minutes. Remove spent grain, and bring wort to a boil. Turn off the heat, and add malt extract syrup, honey, and black malt flour. Stir until completely dissolved, and then return to the heat. Add Nugget hops and 1 ounce Chinook hops. Boil for 90 minutes, adding 0.75 ounce Chinook hops for the final 20 minutes and Irish moss for the final 10 minutes. Cool wort and pitch yeast and yeast nutrient. Ferment 5 to 7 days, and transfer to a secondary fermenter. Ferment an additional 5 to 7 days. Bottle or keg. Age 14 to 21 days before serving.

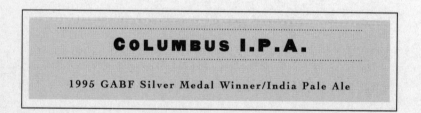

# COLUMBUS I.P.A.

### 1995 GABF Silver Medal Winner/India Pale Ale

9 POUNDS LIGHT MALT EXTRACT SYRUP

2 POUNDS CRYSTAL MALT (120L)

4 OUNCES COLUMBUS HOPS 13.9% ALPHA

1 TEASPOON IRISH MOSS

YEAST NUTRIENT

ALE YEAST

Fill a brewpot with 6 gallons of water, and heat to 165°F. Add crystal malt, and steep for 20 minutes. Remove spent grain, and bring wort to a boil. Turn off heat, and add malt extract syrup. Stir until completely dissolved and return to the heat. Add Columbus hops. Boil for 20 minutes, adding Irish moss for the final 10 minutes. Cool wort and pitch yeast and yeast nutrient. Ferment 4 to 5 days and transfer to a secondary fermenter. Ferment an additional 5 to 7 days. Bottle or keg. Age 10 to 14 days before serving.

> **NOTE:** *Total boil time is 20 minutes. Although this is inefficient, it provides the best flavor.*
> *Columbus is a high-alpha and high-oil hop variety.*

# 8.

## FAL ALLEN

### Pike Place
### Brewing Company

*"I had a minor in beer in college,
as most college students do."*

**F**al Allen's passion for craft beer began in 1982 when he moved from Hawaii to Oregon to attend college. "There wasn't much good beer in Hawaii where I grew up. I finally discovered in Oregon that there was something besides Budweiser." Two years later, he used a Christmas present of $100 to buy a homebrew kit. His homebrewing took a quantum leap in 1987 when a restaurant he had been bartending in caught fire. Although the majority of the damage was smoke damage, the insurance company declared the building a complete loss. Fal was able to "rescue" a wide array of kegs, Cornelius kegs, tap fittings, and carbon dioxide tanks. "I loaded everything I could possibly fit into my Volkswagen van. Technically, all of it belonged to the insurance company, but the insurance rep on the site said, 'Well, whatever's not here in the morning, we won't have to take to the dump.' I felt that I was doing a public service. And the additional equipment allowed me to take homebrewing to a completely new level."

Fal finished school with an education in anthropology and biology, as well as an educated palate. Eventually he realized that brewing was the only career that satisfied all of these interests. With homebrew in hand, he pestered every brewer he knew until Rick Buchanan at Red Hook hired him. Two years later, he moved on to Pike Brewing Company, where he has served as head brewer since 1991. Under his brewing influence, Pike Place has garnered an array of Great American Beer Festival medals. After more than six years as head brewer at Pike, one of the country's most widely known micros, Fal is a well-versed and knowledgeable brewer with a firm grasp on a wide range of styles and what goes into making them.

## THE RIGHT INGREDIENT FOR THE RIGHT BEER

Great beers can be made with practically any ingredients, and there are exceptions to every rule, but let's face it, the ingredients are the heart of the beer, so choosing the right ones goes a long way toward improving your brewing. And what's more germane to your ingredient list than grain?

When selecting grains, one simple principle is that to reproduce the flavors of a region, use the grains from that region. As Fal explains, "When you're buying American malt, you're buying malt that was grown and malted for the big American brewers. That's not to say you can't make some damn good beer with American malt; Sierra Nevada uses it, and their beer is absolutely fabulous. You can make British-style beers with American malt, but I think you really need to go to the source and see what those people are using to get the flavors you want." This is true of specialty grains as well. Fal raised the example of Pike's Bamburg Rauchbier, for which he imported a German smoked malt. "I just didn't see any other way to get that exact flavor that I wanted." When making a regional style of beer, don't stop at just using imported pale malt. Use the same indigenous crystal, chocolate, roasted barley, or whatever else is needed in your beer.

Regarding six-row versus two-row malt, Fal is convinced that two-row malt is far superior to six-row malt. Six-row malt is grainy, needs to be step-mashed to get full efficiency, and lacks the full, round flavors of two-row. This is especially important when making ales. "I would never use six-row malt in an ale," Fal explains. "Six-row malt is produced for making lagers but now even lager brewers are moving away from it."

Munich malt is a particular favorite of Fal for many of his ales. He finds it a versatile malt that adds a nice, malty flavor and some good color. "It gives the beer a subtle roundness."

Although Fal doesn't use adjuncts in any of the beers he currently brews at Pike, he doesn't disapprove of them. "For certain styles, like a malt liquor or an American light lager, I think you have to use an adjunct." Don't be afraid to experiment. Fal fondly recalls a fabulous wild rice beer brewed by former colleague Kelly Meiss, now head brewer at Jefferson State Brewing Company.

When choosing hops, fresh is always best. Pelletized hops are processed soon after being picked and packaged in foil to minimize oxidation. According to Fal, this makes them the most consistently fresh choice. If you want to use whole-leaf hops, buy domestic varieties that have been vacuum packed.

As with grains, indigenous hops are essential for brewing authentic regional-style beers. If you plan to brew British-style beers, be sure to use pellet hops, because it is nearly impossible to get fresh whole-leaf hops imported from Britain.

When dry hopping, Fal extols the virtues of plug hops—compressed-leaf hops. Pellets can be difficult to get out of suspension and may muck up the secondary fermenter. Plugs offer a nice compromise between the freshness of pellets and the form of whole leaf.

Fal points out that big commercial brewers are trying to make beer at the lowest possible cost, and their ingredient selection is driven by economics. Homebrewers working with small batches should not skimp on ingredients. "For a few extra dollars, you can make the best beer possible, so why not do it?"

28 POUNDS ENGLISH 2-ROW PALE MALT

1 POUND ENGLISH CRYSTAL MALT

4 OUNCES CHOCOLATE MALT

4 OUNCES SPECIAL B MALT

1 POUND RAW SUGAR

4 OUNCES GOLDINGS HOPS

ENGLISH ALE YEAST

Mash grains for 90 minutes at 150–152°F. Sparge and collect wort. Add sugar to wort, and boil for 120 minutes, adding the Goldings hops after 60 minutes. Cool wort and pitch yeast. Ferment at 69–72°F for 7 to 20 days. Chill to 55°F, and age an additional 2 to 4 days. Transfer to a secondary fermenter, and age an additional 3 to 4 weeks. Bottle or keg. Age 6 to 12 months before serving.

## OLD BAWDY BARLEY WINE

### Pike Place Pilot Recipe

24 POUNDS ENGLISH 2-ROW LIGHTLY PEATED MALT

6 POUNDS ENGLISH 2-ROW PALE MALT

1 POUND ENGLISH CRYSTAL MALT

8 OUNCES MUNICH MALT

1/4 OUNCE BLACK MALT

4 1/2 OUNCES CHINOOK HOPS

4 OUNCES GOLDINGS HOPS

4 OUNCES CENTENNIAL HOPS

ENGLISH ALE YEAST

Mash grains at 150–152°F for 90 minutes. Sparge and collect wort. Bring wort to a boil, and add Chinook hops. Boil for 90 minutes, adding Golding hops and Centennial hops during the final 5 minutes. Cool wort and pitch yeast. Ferment at 69–72°F for 7 to 10 days. Chill to 55°F, and age 2 to 4 days. Transfer to a secondary fermenter, and age 12 weeks. Bottle or keg. Age 2 to 12 months before serving.

# PORTSIDE PILSNER

17 POUNDS GERMAN 2-ROW PILSNER MALT
1 POUND MUNICH MALT
1 POUND CARA-PILS MALT
3 OUNCES HALLERTAUER HOPS
1 OUNCE TETTNANGER HOPS
3 OUNCES SAAZ HOPS
WYEAST 2208 OR 2007 (OR OTHER LAGER YEAST)

Mash grains at 122°F for 20 to 30 minutes. Transfer the thickest one-third of the mash to another vessel. Add a small amount of water, and bring to a boil. Transfer back to the main mash. Stabilize at 148–150°F for 60 minutes. Transfer the thickest one-third of the mash to another vessel. Add a small amount of water, and bring to a boil. Transfer back to the main mash. Stabilize at 170°F (mash out). Sparge as normal. Bring to a boil and add Hallertauer hops. Boil for 90 minutes, adding Tettnanger hops for the final 10 minutes and Saaz hops at the end of the boil. Cool wort and pitch yeast. Ferment at 50°F for 7 to 10 days. Chill to 45°F, and age 2 to 4 days. Transfer to a secondary fermenter and age an additional 8 to 12 weeks at 35–40°F. Bottle or keg. Age an additional 2 to 4 weeks before serving.

## HOLY ROLLER
## TRAPPIST ALE

18 POUNDS BELGIAN 2-ROW AMBER MALT

1 POUND ENGLISH CRYSTAL MALT

1 POUND MUNICH MALT

2 OUNCES SPECIAL B MALT

2 POUNDS RAW SUGAR

3 OUNCES HERSBRUCKER HOPS

2 OUNCES GOLDINGS HOPS

2 OUNCES HERSBRUKER HOPS

2 OUNCES GOLDINGS HOPS

2 OUNCES HERSBRUKER HOPS

WYEAST 1214 OR OTHER BELGIAN ALE YEAST

Mash grains at 152–154°F for 90 minutes. Boil 90 minutes, and add 3 ounces Hersbrucker hops. Add 2 ounces Hersbrucker and 2 ounces Goldings hops during the final 10 minutes and 2 ounces Hersbrucker and 2 ounces Goldings hops at the end of the boil. Cool wort and pitch yeast. Ferment at 74–78°F for 4 to 7 days. Chill to 50–55°F and age 2 to 4 days. Transfer to a secondary fermenter, and age an additional 2 to 3 weeks. Bottle or keg. Age 2 to 4 weeks before serving.

# 9.

## JIM MIGLIORINI

### Heartland Brewery

*"I approach beer the same way
a chef approaches food."*

Bay leaves, cilantro, white peppercorns, smoked chipotle peppers—not what you would expect to find in a beer recipe. But for Jim Migliorini, brewing is not just about beer. Brewing is about creating and composing. It's an application of years of experience as a chef and a fruit-wine maker, attaining flavor complexities beyond the range of hops, malt, yeast, and water.

Jim began his brewing career at Commonwealth Brewing Company in Boston and is currently the head brewer for Heartland Brewery in New York City. He produces a wide array of beers, from his gold medal-winning and straightforward Farmer Jon's Oatmeal Stout to the incredibly complex Caliente Lager. Jim's culinary talents are most evident in his fruit and herbed and spiced beers.

## Herbed and Spiced Beers

Jim's background affects his approach to herbs and spices repeatedly. When formulating beer recipes, he looks to culinary examples for enticing flavor combinations.

Determining what quantities of herbs and spices to use requires knowledge of the potency of the particular ingredient—much like alpha acids in hops, only more subjective. Again, thinking in terms of cooking is helpful. "I think about it as, 'If I were on a stovetop, how much would I use?'" Jim explains. Jim always uses fresh whole spices because their flavors are more subtle, less variable, and easier to adjust, since they can be removed when the desired potency is reached. Whole spices, like nutmeg, cloves, black pepper, and cinnamon, can be added to the boil. They should be placed in muslin bags and added no sooner than 30 minutes before the end of the boil. Jim often used second and third spice additions, as if they were hops. "I think of it like making tomato sauce. I'll add herbs at the beginning, but the flavors change over the cooking time, so I might add some fresh herbs again near the end."

Some herb and spice additions are made after the boil—either steeped during cooling or as flavoring agents in the conditioning phase, much like dry hopping. Unlike hops, adding herbs and spices during these phases contributes flavor as well as aroma. Jim suggests tasting the developing beer daily to determine flavor, and removing the herbs and spices when the desired profile is reached. "It's like making a dip," Jim suggests. "The flavors develop and intensify with each passing day." As in the boil, herbs and spices should be added in muslin bags for easy removal.

# FRUIT

Fruit and even vegetables are popular additions to beer. In cooking and in brewing, fresh ingredients are the key to quality, with seasonal availability determining selection—for instance, pumpkin in the fall and berries in the summer. Jim feels that freshness is key. Instead of using the popular dried curaçao orange peel, he uses the zest of fresh Valencia oranges, available across the street at the farmers' market.

Attaining a balance between sweet and tart is the goal in cooking and in brewing too. Boiling fruit will release pectins that will cloud beer, and the essential oils become bitter, so Jim recommends using fruit only in the fermentation and conditioning phases. However, starchy vegetables, like pumpkin and winter squash, can be added to the mash for conversion to add fermentables as well as flavor.

Whole fruits are added during secondary fermentation, when the alcohol can draw out flavor and color without releasing undesirable pectins. Cherries and berries should be crushed slightly by hand to break the skins. "Cherry pits are essentially wood and impart tannins," Jim says. They should be added with the fruit when a dry, woody finish is desired. Don't crush the pits, because they will contribute a harsh bitterness. Peaches, plums, and other large fruits should be pitted and slightly pureed—and with the skins on, because they contribute color and aroma.

Jim often uses high-quality fruit concentrates instead of whole fruits, because they are easier to handle and can be less expensive. Fruit extracts, which use alcohol to draw out the fruit flavor, are undesirable because they are astringent and less full flavored. Concentrates should be treated the same as whole fruit and added late in secondary fermentation. Fruit concentrates are available in home winemaking stores. Be sure not to bottle your beer too soon after adding fruit concentrates or juices; fructose is a highly fermentable sugar and may affect carbonation.

When using citrus fruits, only the zest (and never the fruit) should be used. The zest contains essential oils, which contribute their signature flavor and aroma. The zest should be added in the conditioning phase only and never in the boil because it will impart an unpleasant bitterness.

## OTHER FLAVORINGS

Remember that hops are an herb and can be used to complement other flavors. For instance, hops like Cascade, Liberty, and Chinook, which have citrusy characters, accentuate the flavor of citrus fruit beers and balance other sweeter fruit beers.

Wood has traditionally been used to complement the flavors of intoxicating beverages like brandy, port, and scotch and can contribute some wonderful flavors and color to beer, especially fruit beer. Jim extracts the flavor and color from wood chips by placing them in a container of fermented beer. Then this mixture is strained and the liquid added to the beer prior to packaging. Color and flavor can also be extracted from wood by placing them in clear alcohol like vodka. But be aware that this will change the flavor profile and alcohol content of the beer.

# SMILING PUMPKIN ALE

8 3/4 POUNDS PALE 2-ROW AMERICAN MALT

3/4 POUND CRYSTAL MALT (60L)

1 CUP HONEY

1/4 POUND LIGHT BROWN SUGAR

1/4 POUND CORN SUGAR

8 POUNDS WHOLE PUMPKIN

1/2 OUNCE CLUSTER HOPS

1/2 OUNCE CASCADE HOPS

1/4 OUNCE MT. HOOD HOPS

2 TEASPOONS GYPSUM

3 CINNAMON STICKS

2 NUTMEGS (CRUSHED)

3 WHOLE CLOVES

1 TSP WHOLE ALLSPICE

1 TEASPOON KOSHER OR SEA SALT

1 TEASPOON IRISH MOSS

WYEAST 1056 AMERICAN ALE YEAST

Seed and quarter the pumpkin. Place the pieces on a baking sheet and drizzle with honey. Bake at 375°F until tender, about 1 hour. Add the pumpkin to the mash tun with the grains and mash for 60 to 90 minutes at 152°F. Sparge and collect wort. Bring wort to a boil and add all spices. Boil 60 minutes, adding Cluster hops at the beginning of boil and Cascade and Mt. Hood hops and Irish moss during the last 5 minutes. Cool wort and pitch yeast. Ferment at 67°F for 3 to 5 days. Transfer to a secondary fermenter; cool to 55°F. Condition for 5 to 7 days. Cool to 34°F and condition for 1 to 2 days. Bottle or keg. Age 5 to 7 days before serving.

# JACK-O-LANTERN

Jim's culinary background is evident in all of his beers, and especially in his holiday offerings. Jack-O-Lantern is a mix of Smiling Pumpkin ale and cider, served in a glass rimmed with curry-roasted pumpkin seeds. Here is the recipe for the pumpkin seed mixture.

2 CUPS HULLED PUMPKIN SEEDS

3 TABLESPOONS CURRY POWDER

3 TABLESPOONS BROWN SUGAR

1/2 TEASPOON KOSHER SALT

1/2 TEASPOON PEPPER

1/2 TEASPOON PAPRIKA

1/2 TEASPOON GROUND CORIANDER

1/2 TEASPOON GROUND CUMIN

Combine the spices. Coat the pumpkin seeds with peanut oil, and toss them with the spices. Spread the seeds on a cookie sheet, and roast at 325°F for 10 minutes. Place the seeds in a food processor, and grind to a very coarse mixture. Rim a glass with apple cider, and then rim the glass in the pumpkin seed mixture. Fill the glass with two-thirds pumpkin ale and one-third cider. If you don't have a homebrewed cider available, we suggest Blackthorne cider.

# FARMER JON'S
# OATMEAL STOUT

1997 GABF Gold Medal Winner
1995 GABF Bronze Medal Winner

10 POUNDS PALE 2-ROW AMERICAN MALT

1 POUND ROASTED BARLEY

1 POUND FLAKED OATS

1/2 POUND FLAKED BARLEY

1/4 POUND CRYSTAL MALT (20L)

1/4 POUND FLAKED WHEAT

1 OUNCE CLUSTER HOPS

1 OUNCE MT. HOOD HOPS

1/2 OUNCE HALLERTAUER HOPS

2 TEASPOONS GYPSUM

1/4 TEASPOON KOSHER SALT

1 TEASPOON IRISH MOSS

WYEAST 1056 AMERICAN ALE YEAST

## OG: 1.056

Mash grains for 60 minutes at 156°F. Add gypsum to the mash water and sparge. Bring wort to a boil, and add Cluster hops and kosher salt. Boil 90 minutes, adding Hallertauer hops and Irish moss for the final 5 minutes. Cool wort and pitch yeast. Ferment at 67°F for 3 to 5 days. Transfer to a secondary fermenter, and cool to 55°F. Condition 5 to 7 days. Cool to 34°F, and condition 1 to 2 days. Bottle or keg. Age 5 to 7 days before serving.

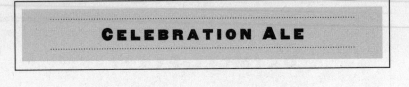

# CELEBRATION ALE

9 POUNDS PALE 2-ROW AMERICAN MALT

1 1/2 POUNDS CRYSTAL MALT (60L)

1/2 POUND CHOCOLATE MALT

1/2 POUND TORREFIED BARLEY

1 OUNCE BLACK PATENT MALT

1/2 OUNCE MT. HOOD HOPS

1/2 OUNCE MT. HOOD HOPS

1/3 OUNCE JUNIPER BERRIES

1/4 OUNCE JUNIPER BERRIES

1/2 OUNCE GINGER

1 CUP PURE MAPLE SYRUP

2 TEASPOONS GYPSUM

1/4 TEASPOON KOSHER SALT

1 TEASPOON IRISH MOSS

WYEAST 1056 AMERICAN ALE YEAST

OG: 1.055

Mash grains for 60 minutes at 156°F. Add gypsum to mash water and sparge. Bring wort to a boil, and add 1/2 ounce Mt. Hood hops and kosher salt. Boil 90 minutes, adding 1/3 ounce juniper berries after 45 minutes; ginger after 80 minutes; and 1/2 ounce Mt. Hood hops, maple syrup, and Irish moss after 85 minutes. Cool wort and pitch yeast. Ferment at 67°F for 3 to 5 days. Transfer to a secondary fermenter, cool to 55°F, and add 1/4 ounce juniper berries. Condition 5 to 7 days. Cool to 34°F, and condition 1 to 2 days. Bottle or keg. Age 5 to 7 days before serving.

# INDIAN RIVER ALE

9 POUNDS PALE 2-ROW AMERICAN MALT

1/2 POUND VICTORY MALT

1/2 POUND CRYSTAL MALT (60L)

1/2 POUND CORN SUGAR

1/2 OUNCE GALENA HOPS

1 OUNCE CASCADE HOPS

1 1/2 OUNCES ORANGE PEEL

1 OUNCE CORIANDER

1 TEASPOON GYPSUM

1/4 TEASPOON KOSHER SALT

1 TEASPOON IRISH MOSS

WYEAST 1056 AMERICAN ALE YEAST

OG: 1.052

Mash grains for 60 minutes at 156°F. Add gypsum to mash water and sparge. Bring wort to a boil, and add Galena hops, corn sugar, and kosher salt. Boil 90 minutes, adding 1/2 ounce orange peel immediately and 1/2 ounce orange peel after 30 minutes. Add Cascade hops, 1/2 ounce orange peel, and Irish moss after 85 minutes. Cool wort and pitch yeast. Ferment at 67°F for 3 to 5 days. Transfer to a secondary fermenter and cool to 55°F. Condition 5 to 7 days. Cool to 34°F degrees, and condition 1 to 2 days. Bottle or keg. Age 5 to 7 days before serving.

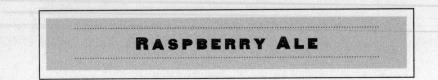

# RASPBERRY ALE

4 1/2 POUNDS PALE 2-ROW AMERICAN MALT

2 1/2 POUNDS WHEAT MALT

1/4 POUND TORREFIED BARLEY

1/4 POUND FLAKED BARLEY

1/4 POUND FLAKED WHEAT

1/2 OUNCE LIBERTY HOPS

1/2 OUNCE LIBERTY HOPS

3 CUPS RASPBERRY SYRUP

1/4 POUND HONEY

1/4 POUND CORN SUGAR

1/4 OUNCE GINGER, CHOPPED FINE

1/8 TEASPOON KOSHER SALT

1 TEASPOON IRISH MOSS

WYEAST 1056 AMERICAN ALE YEAST

OG: 1.045

Mash grains for 60 minutes at 156°F. Add gypsum to mash water and sparge. Bring wort to a boil, and add honey, corn sugar, 1/2 ounce Liberty hops, and kosher salt. Boil 90 minutes, adding ginger after 60 minutes and 1/2 ounce Liberty hops and Irish moss after 85 minutes. Cool wort and pitch yeast. Ferment at 67°F for 3 to 5 days. Transfer to a secondary fermenter, cool to 55°F, and add raspberry syrup. Condition 5 to 7 days. Cool to 34°F, and condition 1 to 2 days. Bottle or keg. Age 5 to 7 days before serving.

# 10.

## GREG NOONAN

### Vermont Pub and Brewery

*"Lager brewing is the touchstone of scientific, well-thought-out, good-practice brewing. You can learn from it, whether you brew lagers or not."*

Greg Noonan, author of *Brewing Lager Beer* (1986) and the recently updated *New Brewing Lager Beer* (1996), founded the Vermont Pub and Brewery in Burlington, Vermont, with his wife, Nancy, in November 1988. In April 1994, Greg opened the Seven Barrel Brewery in West Lebanon, New Hampshire. His latest project is helping to open the Amherst Brewing Company, Amherst, Massachusetts. In 1991 and 1992, the Vermont Pub and Brewery was awarded a bronze medal at the Great American Beer Festival for its Vermont Smoked Porter in the Smoked/Flavored Beers category, and it won a gold medal in 1993 for its Auld Tartan Wee Heavy in the Strong Ale category.

Greg Noonan started homebrewing all grain (he has brewed with extract only twice in his life) and shudders when recalling the first fruits of his labor. "My first grain brews were disasters. I mean they were just awful—grainy, astringent, whoa!" In the early days of his hobby, there was little literature available for the all-grain enthusiast. Before learning about lautering techniques from Fred Eckhardt's A *Treatise on Lager Brewing* and Dave Line's *Big Book of Brewing*, Greg was sparging by putting his mash in cheesecloth and pouring the wort and hot water through it. It was this lack of information that, years later, motivated Greg to write *Brewing Lager Beer*, widely respected as the best lager reference book for home-brewers and professionals.

Lager brewing, and particularly decoction brewing, is sometimes perceived as difficult and intimidating, and in a sense it is: lagers are much less forgiving of the brewer than the bolder, more robust ale family. Greg's early sparging methods resulted in what he now knows is called hot-side aeration. While the broader flavor profile of ales can mask the off-flavors (astringency) produced by splashing wort, the imperfections would be glaring in a light lager. But it was not the challenge or the meticulous practices of the German brewers that drew Greg to decoction mashing. It was fate: "I started decoction mashing because I moved to a house that had an electric stove that was difficult to deal with. I used to do step infusion, but by the time the electric stove came up to heat and I took the mash away, I had missed the mark, so I started decoction mashing. I would put a small pot of grain on the stove and boil it. No problem. I would keep the main mash in a cooler right next to the stovetop and mix it back and forth to get the steps." Decoction mashing was the easiest method to use given the restrictions of his equipment.

Decoction mashing is much simpler for homebrewers than it is for professional brewers. Specialized equipment is required for moving large quantities of mash between the lauter tun and the cereal cooker in a commercial setting, whereas at home, the brewer merely requires an extra pot on the stove. This is not to say that decoction mashing, and lager brewing for that matter, is something you should rush into. Your lager brew should be well thought out. Greg says, "If there is a national character in Germany, the Germans are precise, and German brewing is good practice overall."

German brewers developed decoction mashing to make the most of the grains they had available. Undermodified malts required brewery processing to convert all the starches available. The practice of boiling portions of the mash served to liquefy the starches and provide easier access to the limited enzymes. Modern malting techniques, and the quality of barley available, produce well-modified malt that does not require decoction for conversion. In fact, Greg tells us that if you try decoction mashing with well-modified malt, you will end up with a thin beer. Well-modified malt has a soluble nitrogen ratio (SNR, S/T, or Kolbach index) of 40 or higher. Your malt supplier should be able to provide you with malt specification sheets, which will have these facts as well as other information. If you want to try your hand at decoction, make sure you use undermodified malt with a soluble nitrogen ratio of 33 to 38.

When discussing brewing water, Greg recommends the use of tapwater, as long as it is not totally unpalatable. Boil off chlorine, or filter it out at the faucet. A few beer styles require specific water treatment. Dortmunder-style lagers require "a fair amount of calcium and a fair amount of chloride" (up to 200 ppm of each). Big, hoppy British beers like IPAs and ESBs require hardness proportionate to the hops. If you don't treat your water accordingly, the beer will come out tasting soapy. Greg points out that most beer styles are defined by the water available for brewing in their region of origin. "Edinburgh to London to Burton, and Dortmund to Pilzen—every one of those styles was predicated on the water they had available. Homebrewers don't need to be any different. If your water is really hard, brew hoppy beers. If your water is alkaline, brew dark beers."

Control mash pH by treating your brewing water. Greg recommends a saccharification pH of 5.3 at room temperature. pH varies with temperature, and you will get the most accurate, consistent readings if you test cooled samples. "In general, beers that are more acidic have more flavor. Beers that don't have much acidity tend to be pretty bland." With that in mind, Greg suggests you err on the acidic side. Greg uses lactic acid to adjust pH in his lagers because it has a "rounder flavor." Phosphoric acid, a commonly used alternative, tends to contribute a sharp flavor. "It's great in Coca-Cola, but I don't like it very much in beer."

When mashing in and during decoctions, take care not to introduce too much air into the bed. Hot-side aeration can occur even at this stage, producing biting astringency. Run off slowly, and don't oversparge. Check the gravity of your wort as you transfer it to the brew kettle, and when it drops to a specific gravity of 1.015 to 1.012, stop there. Running off wort below this gravity will result in harsh, undesirable flavors. "It's not worth the risk," warns Greg.

Greg recommends pellet hops in the kettle for their convenience but prefers to use leaf hops in a hop-back to contribute "nice flavor characteristics that you can't get in the boil." He adds hops at the start of the boil to reduce boil-over, but seldom uses 60-minute hop additions because they contribute a coarser bitterness. Additions at 45 minutes and 30 minutes are more subtle. As for varieties, Greg prefers Noble hops when making Czech or European lagers. Cascade makes a nice lager, but it is not appropriate if you are replicating European styles.

Yeast selection and pitching rate are the final influence the brewer will have on the flavor of the lager. A great all-purpose lager yeast that Greg recommends is Weihenstephan 34/70, available from Wyeast. "It's incredibly neutral. It clears well, drops well, ferments pretty quickly. It makes very little contribution to the flavor of the beer." That being said, Greg prefers to use yeast strains that produce pronounced flavors and sometimes blends strains to suit his needs. Greg cites his ideal pilsner — Pilsner Urquell — for being "low in flavor impact, yet well-rounded and crisp." He attributes this unique achievement to the practice of fermenting the wort with two different strains of yeast, which produce individual flavor contributions. Each batch is divided into separate fermenters and pitched separately, and then blended again during cellaring.

When it comes to selecting a yeast strain, it is advisable, but not necessary, to choose a bottom-fermenting variety. Greg says, "Much like a steam beer uses a lager yeast for an ale, there are ale strains that will ferment at low temperatures and yield a lager-like flavor profile. Any yeast that will produce a low amount of esters and a low amount of diacetyl can be suitable for brewing lagers." Greg suggests that you find a yeast strain you like and stick with it. Many ale strains ferment at temperatures of 50°F to 65°F without producing any esters at all.

Pitching yeast is not as simple as smacking the yeast pack the day before you brew. "You can pitch 2 million cells in an ale and get away with it, but if you do that with a lager, it's not going to taste like a lager." The esters that develop as a result of underpitching are readily apparent in delicate lagers. Conversely, in some British ales, the development of esters is an important part of the style profile. Pitching rates for lagers should be on the order of 10 to 14 million cells. To ensure a sufficient pitch volume, make a yeast starter, and double it at least twice (up to 10 percent of the brew volume), or brew often and keep repitching the yeast from recent brews. Greg recommends investing in a yeast collection cap, a device that allows you to turn your carboy into a conical bottomed fermenter by turning it upside down. You can then crop yeast off for pitching and rack the yeast off from under the beer, continuing secondary fermentation in your primary fermenter and thus reducing the risk of infection by never exposing your beer to potential contaminants during transfer. "I've always thought it was the only way to brew lagers," notes Greg.

Finally, lagers take their name from the German practice of cold-conditioning beer in caves for a long period. To make a great lager, you have to be patient. Many breweries lager their beer for 21 days—too short, according to Greg. As a homebrewer, you don't have the pressures that a professional brewer does, and you can afford to make your beer extra special. Two to three months at 30°F to 45°F is just enough, but if you can wait longer, you should. Flavors should peak in 3 to 6 months, depending on the strength of your lager.

## BOMBAY GRAB INDIA ALE

India pale ales (IPAs) were created by nineteenth-century British brewers as export beers for the colonies. The beer needed to travel well and to be refreshing in oppressively hot climates.

Bombay Grab is Vermont Pub and Brewery's IPA, named after the taproom at the Hogdons brewery in London, the creator of the style. This brand relies heavily on a huge floral-and-citrusy bouquet achieved by dry hopping to complement its profound bitterness. The Perles as a finish hop in the kettle or hopback blend with the Cascade aromatics, combining to create a softer aroma.

Dry hops tend to float on the surface, but they can be induced to drop more readily by wetting them first. Using high-temperature water makes a lot of brewers more comfortable, but the wetted hops then need to be added to the secondary fermenter quickly, so they don't lose significant aromatics. A *note of caution:* Adding dry hops to beer invariably causes some foaming. If the hops are wet and hot, it can be like opening a shaken bottle of beer. It is advisable to knock some of the retained carbonation out of the beer before dry hopping.

Water treatment: To 7 gallons of soft water, add:

30 GRAMS (7 1/2 TEASPOONS) GYPSUM
5 GRAMS (1 TEASPOON) EPSOM SALTS

If your water source is not soft, reduce the water salts accordingly to yield very hard, sulfate water of about 750 mg/L hardness.

Crush:

8 POUNDS PALE MALT

1/2 POUND WHEAT MALT

1/2 POUND CARA-PILS MALT

1/3 POUND CRYSTAL MALT (50L)

Mash the grains at 152°F for 1 hour with 2 1/2 gallons liquor at 169°F. Sparge with 3 3/4 gallons liquor at 174°F, adding the runoff to 3/4 of a gallon of liquor in the wort kettle. Boil the wort for 90 minutes.

Add the hops:

2 1/4 AAUs (ALPHA ACID UNITS) OF CASCADE HOPS
AT THE START OF THE BOIL

22 AAUs OF CASCADE HOPS TO BOIL FOR 45 MINUTES

15 AAUs OF CASCADE HOPS TO BOIL FOR 30 MINUTES

Add:

1/2 OUNCE PERLE HOPS TO THE WORT AFTER SHUTTING OFF
THE HEAT UNDER THE KETTLE

Pitch with:

7–10 GRAMS (6–10 MILLION CELLS/MILLILITER) OF FRUITY,
ESTERY ALE YEAST, TO A WELL-AERATED WORT AT 68°F

Ferment out at 72–75°F for 3 days.

Within 3 days of the end of the primary ferment and at least 1 week before bottling, wet 1 3/4 ounces of Cascade hops with 175°F water, and add to the secondary fermenter with the green beer. After 1 to 2 weeks conditioning on the hops, bottle the batch. Prime the beer with 1/2–2/3 cup of corn sugar, depending on your carbonation preference.

OG: 1.052 • FG: 1.014 • Color: 8 SRM
Bitterness: 75 IBU • 5% ABV

# SLEEPWALKER
# BARLEYWINE

**B**arleywines should be big and intense. The intensity is achieved by the high alcohol content, the big bitterness, and the huge bouquet of esters and higher alcohols from the fast, warm ferment.

This recipe calls for a mash combined with 2 kilograms of malt extract added to the wort kettle to achieve its high initial gravity. To brew an all-grain version, add 4 3/4 more pounds of pale malt, increase the mash and sparge liquor volumes by 1 gallon each, and boil the wort intensely for 2 hours (add 30 minutes to the boil before adding the first hops) to evaporate off excess volume.

Most strains of brewing yeast will ferment even this strong a beer to completion without faltering if enough yeast is pitched, but the yeast usually can't be repitched in a subsequent brew. The brewer needs to be more concerned that enough yeast is pitched, and should choose the particular strain of yeast for its flavor contributions, rather than for its historic use in high-gravity brewing.

Water treatment: To 7 gallons of soft water, add:

11 GRAMS (2 3/4 TEASPOONS) GYPSUM
5 GRAMS (1 TEASPOON) EPSOM SALTS

If your water source is not soft, reduce the water salts accordingly to yield sulfate liquor of about 400 mg/L hardness.

Crush:

7 1/2 POUNDS PALE MALT

1 1/2 POUNDS WHEAT MALT

2 1/4 POUNDS CRYSTAL MALT (50L)

Mash the grains at 150°F for 1 hour with 3 gallons of liquor at 166°F. Sparge with 4 1/4 gallons of liquor at 174°F. Add to:

4.4 POUNDS LIGHT MALT SYRUP IN THE WORT KETTLE

Boil the wort for 90 minutes. Add the hops:

7 AAUs NUGGET HOPS AT THE START OF THE BOIL

11 AAUs NUGGET HOPS TO BOIL FOR 45 MINUTES

2 AAUs FUGGLES HOPS TO BOIL FOR 30 MINUTES

Add:

1 OUNCE FUGGLES HOPS TO THE WORT AFTER SHUTTING OFF
THE HEAT UNDER THE KETTLE

Cool the wort to 65–68°F, and aerate it well as the wort is pitched. Pitch with:

14–21 GRAMS (12–20 MILLION CELLS/MILLILITER) OF A WOODY,
ESTERY ALE YEAST

Ferment out at 68 – 75°F for 5 days.

Within 3 days of the end of the primary ferment, transfer to a secondary fermenter. Condition at below 65°F for at least 2 weeks. Two weeks before bottling, wet 1 ounce of Fuggles hops with 175°F water, and add the hops to the beer in a secondary fermenter. After

1 to 2 weeks conditioning on the hops, bottle the batch. Prime the beer with 1/3 to 1/2 cup of corn sugar, depending on your carbonation preference. Let this beer condition in the bottle for at least 6 months. It needs time for its character to develop.

OG: 1097 • FG: 1024 • Color: 15 SRM
Bitterness: 75 IBU • 9.5% ABV

# WEE HEAVY

**S**cotch ales are relatively mellow, given their high gravity. A low initial fermentation temperature, low bitterness, high terminal gravity, and intensive cellaring are important elements of the style. Caramelizing a bit of wort in the kettle also contributes to an authentic character.

This recipe is for a double-mash brew; the first half of the runoff from each mash is combined for the Wee Heavy wort, and the late runoffs are combined to make an 80-Shilling export wort. The 80-Shilling ale can follow the Wee Heavy into the kettle and be boiled on top of the "spent" hops, because the high-gravity boil of the Wee Heavy leaves plenty of un-isomerized alpha acids to bitter the second brew.

Plan to age the beer. At the Vermont Pub and Brewery, we generally find that our Wees reach maturity after about 10 months at 40°F.

Water treatment for each mash: To 7 1/4 gallons of soft water, add:

4 GRAMS (1 TEASPOON) GYPSUM

2 GRAMS (2/3 TEASPOON) CALCIUM CHLORIDE

If your water source is not soft, reduce the water salts accordingly to yield liquor of about 200–250 mg/L hardness.

Crush:

12 1/3 POUNDS PALE MALT

1/4 POUND ROAST BARLEY

Mash the grains in a thick mash at 158°F for 1 hour with 3 1/4 gallons liquor at 176°F. Sparge with 4 gallons of liquor at 174°F. Boil the wort for 90 minutes. Add the hops:

7 AAUs GOLDINGS OR FUGGLES HOPS AT THE START
OF THE BOIL

2 1/2 AAUs OF GOLDINGS OR FUGGLES HOPS TO BOIL
FOR 45 MINUTES

Add:

1/2 OUNCE GOLDINGS OR FUGGLES HOPS TO THE WORT AFTER
SHUTTING OFF THE HEAT UNDER THE KETTLE

Cool the wort to 60°F, and aerate it moderately well as the wort is pitched. Pitch with:

20–25 GRAMS (18–25 MILLION CELLS/MILLILITER) OF A MILD,
NEUTRAL ALE YEAST

Ferment out at 65–68°F for 6 to 7 days.

Condition at below 60°F. Prime the beer with 1/3 to 1/2 cup corn sugar, depending on your carbonation preference. Let this beer further condition in the bottle for 1 to 2 months, or longer if possible.

WEE HEAVY: OG: 1097 • FG: 1024 • COLOR: 15 SRM
BITTERNESS: 75 IBU • 9.5% ABV
80-SHILLING EXPORT: OG: 1042
FG: 1014 • 4% ABV

## BOHEMIAN PILSNER

**D**ecoction mashing is a dated, time-and-energy-intensive brewhouse program designed to deal with undermodified malts. It would have been relegated to an interesting bit of brewing history a long time ago if it weren't for the fact that it is the only way to extract the sort of profound maltiness that one finds in Bohemian pilsners and Munich helles. This single-decoction mash yields that malty flavor.

Decoction mashing, and protein rests in general, require that the malt be undermodified (SNR - S/T of 33–38). Usual malts, with a soluble nitrogen ratio (SNR) of 42 to 50, will lose too much of their head-and-body proteins in a protein rest, and the beer will be thin. The decoction itself should be thick, and stirred as it heats to boiling to prevent burning.

*Lager* means "to age." Modern temperature control can reduce the time required for a lager to mellow, but even at 30°F, 4 or 5 weeks are required for a lager's flavor to round out.

Water source: Soft water preferred. Add 1 milliliter 85–88 percent lactic acid to 6 3/4 gallons of soft water to adjust its acidity, so that the mash pH will be 5.2 to 5.3.

Crush:

8 3/4 POUNDS PILSNER MALT

Mash the grains in at 131°F with 2 3/4 gallons liquor at 143°F. Remove 1 3/4 gallons of the thickest part of the mash. (Don't take any free-standing liquid along. The 2 3/4 gallon decoction should be composed of about 4 1/2 pounds of malt and 1 to 1 1/4 gallons of liquor.) Cover the main mash to hold its temperature, and begin heating the decoction, taking about 15 minutes to reach 160°F. Heat to boiling while stirring. Boil the decoction for 15 minutes. Mix the two mashes for a dextrinizing rest at 158–160°F for 30 to 45 minutes. Sparge with 3 3/4 gallons of liquor at 174°F. Add 1 1/2 quarts liquor to bring the kettle volume up to 5 3/4 gallons at the start of the boil.

Boil the wort for 90 minutes. Add the hops:

6 3/4 AAUs SAAZ HOPS AT THE START OF THE BOIL

4 1/4 AAUs SAAZ HOPS TO BOIL FOR 45 MINUTES

Add:

1/2 OUNCE SAAZ HOPS TO THE WORT AFTER SHUTTING OFF THE
HEAT UNDER THE KETTLE

Cool the wort to 45°F, and aerate it moderately well as the wort is pitched. Pitch with:

10–14 GRAMS (12–14 MILLION CELLS/MILLILITER) OF
A LAGER YEAST

Ferment out at 48–55°F for 6 to 7 days.

Condition the beer for at least 4 weeks at below 50°F. Prime the beer with 3/4 cup corn sugar.

OG: 1048 • FG: 1014 • COLOR: 3.5 SRM

BITTERNESS: 37 IBU • 4.5% ABV

# 11.

## PAUL SAYLER

### Commonwealth Brewing Company

*"When handling yeast, you try to be graceful and quick. Unfortunately, those two rarely go together."*

Paul Sayler started homebrewing while he was studying microbiology at Hampshire College. His passion melded with his studies when he decided to focus on energy metabolism in brewer's yeast. A brief field study at Catamount Brewing Company in White River Junction, Vermont, led to an assistant brewer position after graduation in 1990. Late in 1995, Paul left his job as assistant brewmaster at Catamount to become the head brewer at the Commonwealth Brewing Company in New York City, where he brews a wide range of beer styles. As a microbiologist, Paul is confident enough to use four or more different strains of yeast concurrently in his brewpub, quite unusual in a commercial brewery or brewpub.

### YEAST

Yeast is the most important brewing ingredient. Not only does it transform malt-sugar water into alcohol and carbon dioxide, thus making it beer, it provides many of the signature flavors in an array of styles. Fruit, sulfur, and butterscotch flavors and aromas—all of these are by-products of yeast. But for all of its power and diversity, it is the most delicate and unstable ingredient. Quite an amazing single-cell organism.

The choice of a yeast strain is usually dictated by the style of beer to be brewed. Select a strain that will produce the characteristics you require for the style. Dry yeast is often unpredictable, and if you are going to maintain a yeast culture, you should spend the extra dollars for a liquid strain.

Pitching an adequate amount of yeast is essential. Paul identifies underpitching as one of the biggest problems for homebrewers. "Give the yeast a fighting chance," Paul asserts. "Get that yeast started!"

Making a starter, for ale or lager yeast, is as simple as making a small quantity of wort the day before you brew and pitching your fresh yeast culture (e.g., an activated Wyeast gold foil packet) into it. Paul advises, "You're looking for a quart to a half-gallon of 1.040 to 1.048 wort." Boil 3/4 cup dry malt extract in 1 quart of water for 5 minutes to dissolve and sterilize the extract. Then cool to room temperature—covered, of course. Sanitize a container at least twice the size of your solution, pour in the cooled wort, and pitch the yeast, all the while paying close attention to cleanliness. Shake well to aerate the starter. Allow the solution to ferment at room temperature for 1 day before the brew. For stronger beers, above 16 Plato, step up the volume of your starter to at least 1/2 gallon.

Paul recommends pitching ale yeast into the finished wort at 62–65°F and aerating well. Let the wort warm naturally to its fermentation temperature of 68°F. A few Belgian and British yeast strains perform best in the low 70s, but most ale strains perform best at 68°F. Certain strains produce desirable fruity esters above 68°F, while others may produce unpleasant esters and higher alcohols above that temperature. Know what characteristics you will get from the yeast when determining your fermentation temperature. Paul advocates experimenting to find the characteristics you like. When brewing

Commonwealth's Hefe-weizen, Paul pitches the yeast at 55°F and allows the fermentation temperature to rise to 65°F. "I wanted a character from the yeast that's more complex than banana. I wanted some vanilla. I got a more interesting character pitching at a lower temperature."

Ale fermentation should be complete in 4 to 5 days. At this point, most professionals perform a diacetyl rest for 12 to 24 hours, to allow the yeast to reabsorb the diacetyl, perceived as a butterscotch flavor, created over the course of fermentation. Homebrewers need to watch the changing gravity of their wort, because not all homebrew fermentations go as smoothly as those in breweries. High-gravity beers, like old ales and barleywines, require a longer rest because there is more than just diacetyl to reabsorb. "By the time the yeast finishes fermenting those alcohols, it's starting to choke. It produces some stuff that you would never taste from that yeast normally. The yeast will reabsorb those if you give it some time to do that." Any ale over 1.060 OG should be warm-conditioned for 7 to 10 days after full attenuation. For example, Paul conditions his Old Ale for 10 days at 60°F, before cooling it to 42°F for extended conditioning.

Lager ferments generally between 40 and 50°F for 5 to 11 days, and is then cold-conditioned (lagered) for up to 10 weeks—ideally, even longer for most pilsners and bocks—at temperatures as low as 32°F. This cold conditioning allows the yeast to reabsorb the esters and sulfur produced during fermentation. Some lager yeast, like the classic pilsner strain, should always begin initial fermentation at temperatures in the low 40s and then be cooled to the low 30s. As with ale yeast, the temperature at which you ferment influences the flavor profile and will vary from strain to strain. Generally lager yeasts create unpleasant characteristics during fermentation, which will become muted during cold conditioning. "The warmer you ferment a lager—55 degrees, for example—the weirder and fouler it's going to be at the end of that fermentation, and as a result, more of that funkiness is going to have to come out in conditioning. You could ferment it colder—say, 45 degrees—which will take a few days longer, but you will have less funkiness that you need to take out by lagering it forever. So it's a trade-off."

Get in the habit of tasting your beer as soon as it reaches full attenuation. You will learn to perceive the characteristics of the yeast that become less identifiable in the fully conditioned beer. Paul opines, "The best way to judge your errors is to taste your beer over time. Those characters are a lot stronger right after fermentation, and if you wait until your beer gets to the bottle, you might not notice it."

Did you ever wonder what would happen if you blended two or more yeast strains? Paul tells us, "I would explore it. Some of the most interesting strains in the world are multistrain yeasts." In fact, many breweries that formerly used multistrain yeasts have switched to single strains, and the question that must be asked is, What has been lost? Although Paul encourages this experimentation, as a scientist he emphasizes record keeping and notes. If you do blend two strains, you should also brew control batches with the original single strains to determine the characteristics you achieve from the blend. Saving this blended strain is not a good idea; one strain eventually will dominate, and you won't be able to recreate the characteristics you achieved in the first batch.

Yeast from most beers can be repitched very sucessfully. However, yeast from beers that contain a large amount of dark grain, like stouts or porters, should not be repitched. Beers with an OG of 16 Plato or more should not be repitched, since the yeast will be too tired to work well in subsequent batches. Also be aware that repeated repitching over many generations will naturally result in genetic mutations to your yeast strain.

Yeast, when handled with care, is the only brewing ingredient that can be used again and again. Harvesting, propagating, and repitching your yeast should be done with the utmost attention to sanitation. Heat-sanitize your vessels (utensils, etc.) at 180°F or above for at least 10 minutes. Anything that can be boiled should be. All containers and work surfaces that cannot be heat-sanitized must be chemically sanitized with an iodine or bleach solution.

Removing vectors—airborne elements that carry organisms that may infect your yeast—is another key to sanitation. "The most common household vector is dust. Reduce dust to a minimum. Vacuum the day before, and make sure there is nothing to move the air around."

Try to move "quickly with grace" while handling the yeast to minimize the time and amount of vectors the yeast is exposed to. Depending on the type of fermenter you are using, there will be different ways of harvesting your yeast. Open-top fermenters, like plastic buckets, allow you simply to scoop the freshest, most viable yeast from the top. Closed fermenters require harvesting the yeast from the bottom of the fermenter in a beer-yeast mixture known as slurry. If you have a glass carboy, the best way to store yeast is to leave it in the carboy after fermentation with a layer of fermented beer as protection, and move the entire vessel to cold storage. This is the most advantageous setup, because each time you transfer yeast, you expose it to possible contamination. When you must move the yeast to another sanitary container for storage, do so with care, and place it in cold storage (33–37°F) as quickly as possible.

Healthy yeast strains are pitched at a rate of approximately $10^6$ cells per milliliter per degree Plato. In larger breweries, this works out to 1 pound per barrel (31 gallons). Ale strains will keep in cold storage from 7 to 14 days and still provide an adequate pitching rate. Beyond 2 weeks, the viability, or ratio of living cells, may have dropped as low as, or even lower than, 30 percent. Viability is an indication of how much living yeast is available to be pitched. For example, if your yeast is 50 percent viable, you will have to pitch twice as much yeast to get a sufficient cell count. A variety of factors influence viability: long periods on the beer after fermentation is complete, overly warm fermentation temperatures, warm storage temperatures, and a variety of factors from the previous fermentation.

For those of you with a little extra money to spend—around $200 to $400—a used microscope and hemocytometer will allow you to check the condition and exact viability of your yeast. A hemocytometer is simply a microscope slide with a microscopic grid calibrated to the millionth of a milliliter. Place a streak of yeast on the slide, and then count the number of viable cells in a random sampling of squares, times 1 million. Another option with yeast is to create a bank of yeast slants to preserve a particularly strong or effective strain.

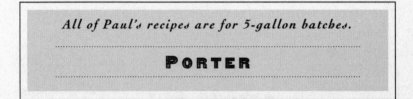

*All of Paul's recipes are for 5-gallon batches.*

## PORTER

8 1/2 POUNDS PALE 2-ROW MALT

11 OUNCES CRYSTAL MALT (60–80L)

4 1/2 OUNCES BLACK BARLEY*

1 1/2 OUNCES CHOCOLATE MALT

1 OUNCE BLACK MALT

1 OUNCE ROASTED BARLEY

5 OUNCES FLAKED BARLEY

1/2 OUNCE EAST KENT GOLDINGS HOPS

1/3 OUNCE CASCADE HOPS

1/3 OUNCE EAST KENT GOLDINGS HOPS

3/4 OUNCE CHALLENGER HOPS

WYEAST LONDON ALE YEAST

OG: 13.2 PLATO

* Black barley, not black patent malt.

Mash grains at 152–153°F for 60 minutes. Sparge and collect wort. Boil for 90 minutes, adding 1/2 ounce East Kent Goldings hops after 10 minutes and 1/3 ounce Cascade and 1/3 ounce East Kent Goldings hops after 75 minutes. Remove from heat and add Challenger hops. Let steep for 15 minutes. Cool wort to 68°F and pitch yeast. Ferment for 5 to 7 days. Transfer to a secondary fermenter, and cool to 42–45°F. Condition an additional 5 to 7 days. Bottle or keg. Age 7 to 10 days before serving.

## STICKE ALT

8 POUNDS PILSNER MALT
8 1/2 OUNCES DEWOLF COSYNS CARAMUNICH MALT
3 1/2 OUNCES DEWOLF COSYNS CARAVIENNE MALT
1 OUNCE CHOCOLATE MALT
3/4 OUNCE BLACK PATENT MALT
.80 OUNCE GERMAN HALLERTAUER MITTEL HOPS
.30 OUNCE GERMAN HALLERTAUER HOPS
.40 OUNCE CZECH SAAZ HOPS
.70 OUNCE CZECH SAAZ HOPS
1/2 OUNCE SPALT HOPS
WYEAST ALT YEAST

OG: 12.2 PLATO

Mash in grains very thick, with 1 1/2–2 gallons of water, at 118–120°F for 30 minutes. Infuse with 210°F water to raise temperature to 145°F. Let rest for 20 minutes. Add more water to raise the temperature to 156°F, and let rest for 40 minutes. Sparge and collect wort. Boil 90 minutes, adding .80 ounce German Hallertauer hops after 10 minutes and .30 ounce German Hallertauer hops and .40 ounce Czech Saaz hops after 75 minutes. Remove from heat and add .70 ounce Czech Saaz hops. Let steep for 15 minutes. Cool wort to 62°F and pitch yeast. Let temperature rise to 65°F, and ferment for 5 to 7 days. Transfer to a secondary fermenter, and cool to 34–36°F. Condition for 1 month, adding Spalt hops for the final 7 to 10 days. Bottle or keg. Age 7 to 10 days before serving.

## NUT BROWN ALE

7 1/2 POUNDS PALE 2-ROW MARIS OTTER MALT

11 1/2 OUNCES CRYSTAL MALT (60L)

3 OUNCES PALE CHOCOLATE MALT*

.50 OUNCE CHOCOLATE MALT

1.3 OUNCES BROWN MALT*

4.5 OUNCES FLAKED BARLEY

1 3/4 OUNCES STYRIAN GOLDINGS HOPS

.60 OUNCE FUGGLES HOPS

WYEAST ENGLISH ALE YEAST

OG: 12.5 PLATO

* Paul obtains pale chocolate malt and brown malt from Beeston malt. Ask your local homebrew supply shop to obtain these malts for you. They are essential to this beer.

Mash grains at 151°F for 60 minutes. Sparge and collect wort. Boil for 90 minutes, adding Styrian Goldings hops after 10 minutes and Fuggles hops after 85 minutes. Cool wort to 68°F and pitch yeast. Ferment for 5 to 7 days. Transfer to a secondary fermenter, and cool to 42–50°F. Condition 4 to 5 days. Bottle or keg. Age 7 to 10 days before serving.

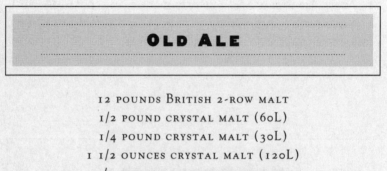

## OLD ALE

12 POUNDS BRITISH 2-ROW MALT

1/2 POUND CRYSTAL MALT (60L)

1/4 POUND CRYSTAL MALT (30L)

1 1/2 OUNCES CRYSTAL MALT (120L)

1 1/2 OUNCES PALE CHOCOLATE MALT

1 OUNCE CHOCOLATE MALT

1 OUNCE EAST KENT GOLDINGS HOPS

2/3 OUNCE CASCADE HOPS

2/3 OUNCE EAST KENT GOLDINGS HOPS

2/3 OUNCE CHALLENGER HOPS

1/3 OUNCE CASCADE HOPS

LONDON ALE YEAST

OG: 1.070

Mash grains at 154°F for 90 minutes. Sparge and collect wort. Boil for 90 minutes, adding 1 ounce East Kent Goldings hops and 2/3 ounce Cascade hops after 10 minutes, and then adding 2/3 ounce East Kent Goldings hops, 2/3 ounce Challenger hops, and 1/3 ounce Cascade hops for the last 5 minutes. Cool wort and pitch yeast. Ferment for 5 to 7 days. Transfer to a secondary fermenter, allowing for a 7-day rest at 58 to 60°F. Bottle or keg. This is an ideal beer to cask-condition. Condition for a minimum of 3 months; 4 months is better, 6 to 8 months is ideal. Don't condition for more than 12 months.

# 12.

## DAN ROGERS

### Holy Cow! Brewpub and Casino

*"When I told the guys at the local homebrew shop that I was going to be the brewer here, they all laughed at me. A few months later, I had a gold medal from GABF, so they were all eating their words."*

**D**an Rogers was a chef in Las Vegas when he learned that the restaurant group he worked for was going to open a brewpub and casino called Holy Cow! A fervent but fairly unseasoned home-brewer, the phrase echoed in Dan's head. He approached owner Tom Wiesner and wowed him with some technical beer jargon like "original gravity" and "step mashing." Don secured the job as head brewer.

As a homebrewer, Dan had brewed only extract batches. But after only five months of all-grain brewing at Holy Cow! Dan took home a Great American Beer Festival gold medal. He then proceeded to take medals three out of Holy Cow!'s first four years in business: a gold for the Pale Ale in 1993, a bronze for the Red Ale in 1994, and a bronze for the Stout in 1996. Dan's skillful brewing instincts, founded on his culinary background and honed by his submersion into a 7-day brewing schedule for Vegas's first and most successful brewpub, are aptly demonstrated by his innovations in technique and equipment and by attention to flavor.

Dan brews an excellent Oatmeal Stout at Holy Cow!, and working with oatmeal poses certain challenges. Dan performs a step infusion/decoction mash for his Oatmeal Stout. He steeps equal parts oatmeal and pale malt at 132 degrees for an hour, then brings the mixture almost to a boil, so that the oatmeal begins to gelatinize. He thens combines this with the rest of the mash, which has been raised to a previously calculated temperature, so that the combined mashes will be at a mashing temperature of 156 degrees.

Dan has also explored different mashing techniques for rye. Rye beers are popular with Dan's customers because they are light bodied and clear, but rye is notoriously sticky in the mash and has low diastatic power. When using rye malt, always make sure you have a good, thick bed of two-row before you blend in the rye malt. Laying down a small bed of six-row can also be helpful because the extra husk from the six-row will help to filter the wort during sparge.

Another technique Dan recommends for upgrading brewing efficiency is a simple yet effective tip for gathering yeast. After the beer has completed primary fermentation and been allowed sufficient time for the diacetyl to be reabsorbed by the yeast, drop the temperature of the beer and rack it off the yeast for collection. "A lot of the most active and viable yeast is still suspended in the beer. By dropping the temperature, you force trub, hop particles, and some dead yeast to drop out. You're harvesting more viable yeast," Dan explains.

Our meeting with Dan also produced the concept for the hop tea chamber, a piece of equipment we now consider indispensable. At Holy Cow! Dan created his own version of a hop-back in a Cornelius keg. He hand-sewed a stainless steel window screen into a cylindrical basket and fastenable lid that fits inside the corni keg. He fills the basket with his aroma hops, then steeps them for 10 minutes, before using the corni keg's in and out valves to sparge the "hop tea" into the fermenter with the fresh wort. Directions for constructing a homebrew-scaled version of this system can be found in Appendix A.

With Dan's brewing and culinary experience, it's no surprise that he has developed a demanding palate. Close attention to the flavors in his beers is a hallmark of his brewing skills. This, of course, affects his choice of ingredients. Perle hops are a current favorite, and he strongly recommends their use for homebrewers, identifying them as highly stable with a true European character, rare in hops of American origin. "I use them for both aroma and bittering," Dan asserts. "They're great all-around hops."

Although Dan is not a big fan of fruit beers personally, Holy Cow! often sells a barrel of fruit beer a night, so Dan has had a lot of experience brewing them. He speaks fondly of the Reinheitsgebot and is clearly somewhat of a purist at heart, preferring traditional fruits in unobtrusive amounts. "I stick mostly to raspberries and blueberries. I also brew a lemon cream ale with lemon rind and coriander— very subtle."

Dan uses multiple yeast strains at Holy Cow!—further evidence of his close attention to flavor. He refuses to use any finings, declaring that he can taste them in the finished product. "If you chill your beer down, the solids will drop out, and it should drop clear. You don't need the finings," Dan opines.

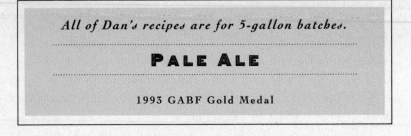

# PALE ALE

### 1993 GABF Gold Medal

8 3/4 POUNDS PALE 2-ROW MALT

3/4 POUND CARAMEL MALT (40L)

3/4 POUND MUNICH MALT

1 1/4 OUNCES FUGGLES HOPS

1 1/4 OUNCES FUGGLES HOPS

1 1/4 OUNCES CASCADE HOPS

5 OUNCES CASCADE HOPS, WHOLE LEAF

WYEAST 1007 OR 1056 YEAST

OG: 1.056 • FG: 1.014

Mash grains at 152–155°F for 60 minutes. Sparge and collect wort. Bring wort to a boil, and add 1 1/4 ounces Fuggles hops. Boil for 60 minutes, adding 1 1/4 ounces Fuggles hops after 30 minutes and 1 1/4 ounces Cascade hops during the final 5 minutes. As wort comes to a boil, place 5 ounces whole-leaf Cascade hops in the hop tea chamber and fill with 160°F water. Set aside. When the boil is complete, drain the hop tea into a separate vessel and siphon hot wort through hops in the hop tea chamber. Cool wort to 65–68°F and pitch yeast. Ferment for 5 to 7 days at 65–68°F. Transfer to a secondary fermenter, and ferment an additional 7 days. Drop the temperature to 45°F for the final 2 days of secondary conditioning. Bottle or keg. Age 5 to 7 days before serving.

# RED ALE

## 1994 GABF Bronze Medal

7 1/2 POUNDS PALE 2-ROW MALT

3/4 POUND CARAMEL MALT (60L)

3/4 POUND CARAMEL MALT (80L)

3/4 POUND CARA-PILS MALT

1/8 POUND ROASTED BARLEY

5/8 OUNCE FUGGLES HOPS

5/8 OUNCE FUGGLES HOPS

1 1/4 OUNCES FUGGLES HOPS

WYEAST 1007 OR 1056 YEAST

OG: 1.056 • FG: 1.016

Mash grains at 152–155°F for 60 minutes. Sparge and collect wort. Bring wort to a boil, and add 5/8 ounce Fuggles hops. Boil for 60 minutes, adding 5/8 ounce Fuggles hops after 30 minutes and 1 1/4 ounces Fuggles hops during the final 5 minutes. Cool wort to 65–68°F and pitch yeast. Ferment for 5 to 7 days at 65–68°F. Transfer to a secondary fermenter, and ferment an additional 7 days. Drop the temperature to 45°F for the final 2 days of secondary conditioning. Bottle or keg. Age 5 to 7 days before serving.

8 POUNDS PALE 2-ROW MALT

1 3/4 POUNDS MUNICH MALT (10L)

1 3/4 POUNDS ROASTED BARLEY

1/2 POUND CARAMEL MALT (120L)

5/8 OUNCE CHINOOK HOPS

5/8 OUNCE CHINOOK HOPS

5/8 OUNCE CHINOOK HOPS

WYEAST 1007 OR 1056 YEAST

OG: 1.060 • FG: 1.020

Mash grains at 152–155°F for 60 minutes. Sparge and collect wort. Bring wort to a boil, and add 5/8 ounce Chinook hops. Boil for 60 minutes, adding 5/8 ounce Chinook hops after 30 minutes and 5/8 ounce Chinook hops during the final 5 minutes. Cool wort to 65–68°F and pitch yeast. Ferment for 5 to 7 days at 65–68°F. Transfer to a secondary fermenter, and ferment an additional 7 days. Drop the temperature to 45°F for the final 2 days of secondary conditioning. Bottle or keg. Age 5 to 7 days before serving.

# HEFE WEIZEN

5 POUNDS PALE 2-ROW MALT

5 POUNDS WHEAT MALT

5/8 OUNCE TETTNANGER HOPS

5/8 OUNCE TETTNANGER HOPS

5/8 OUNCE TETTNANGER HOPS

WYEAST 3068 YEAST

OG: 1.050 • FG: 1.012

Mash grains at 152–155°F for 60 minutes. Sparge and collect wort. Bring wort to a boil and add 5/8 ounce Tettnanger hops. Boil for 60 minutes, adding 5/8 ounce Tettnanger hops after 30 minutes and 5/8 ounce Tettnanger hops during the final 5 minutes. Cool wort to 70–72°F and pitch yeast. Ferment for 5 to 7 days at 70–72°F. Transfer to a secondary fermenter, and ferment an additional 7 days. Drop the temperature to 45°F for the final 2 days of secondary conditioning. Bottle or keg. Age 5 to 7 days before serving.

# 13.

## JOHN MAIER

*Rogue Brewing Company*

*"I do all the nasty stuff. I'm really
proud of that."*

**H**ead brewer at the Rogue Brewery in Newport, Oregon, since 1989, John Maier started his brewing career in 1982 as a home-brewer. Like most of us, he began by making his own beer from ex-tract. In those early days, the prospect of concocting a brew from all grain seemed overwhelming. The idea of mixing 8 pounds of malted barley with steaming water was not appealing when he was winning awards by opening cans of syrup.

After a few years, and a few awards in local and state competi-tion, John started to feel the constraints imposed by brewing with extracts. He had joined a club and found that one member brewed beers that were head and shoulders above the rest. "This guy brewed with all grain and had even cultivated his own yeast." John figured, "If he can do it, why can't I?" With the help of a friend, John put together an all-grain setup that most of us would die for.

A modified Sankey keg for mashing, a large propane burner, a drilled-out cooler for lautering, and a wort chiller changed John

Maier's life. With his brewery set up on the deck of his southern California apartment, John set about becoming the American Homebrewers Association's Homebrewer of the Year 1988 long before he won the award. John's passion for beer was not to be deterred, even by work. Before his shift as an electronics technician, John would mash his grains and run off his wort, then partially boil it before heading off to work, leaving his brewpot securely covered. The next day, he would finish the brew by boiling and hopping the wort and starting fermentation. (And you thought *you* had a long brewday.)

Part of being a good brewer is being creative. Don't be afraid to try something new. Everyone has had a bad batch, and John Maier has dumped his share. "Most," he said, "were due to contamination of the dry yeast strain I used." Switching to a liquid yeast strain solved that problem. Contamination risk can also be minimized by switching to all grain. The wort produced from a mash contains more essential yeast nutrients than that from extract, resulting in a quicker start to fermentation. With that in mind, it is fairly difficult to ruin a batch with your grain bill. The worst that can happen is that you don't achieve the style you were aiming for. John's philosophy is, "When in doubt, add more hops." Those of us familiar with Rogue beers don't doubt that John knows what he is doing.

Hailing from the Pacific Northwest, John prefers to use American hops for their dramatic flavor and aroma, but he is not averse to importing hops as well. John lets loose his creative side annually at Rogue by featuring the latest and greatest hops in Rogue Mogul, a very hoppy Strong Ale brewed every fall. Mogul features six different varieties of hops, which John selects "to use up what we might still have around." His latest favorite hop variety is Crystal. This low-alpha hop is excellent for flavoring and aroma, contributing citrus notes. But it also is excellent for bittering. John used 3 pounds per barrel in his Brutal Bitter (akin to using more than 7.5 ounces in a 5-gallon batch).

Other varieties that he likes to use are Cascade, naturally; Perle, "a good aroma hop that is not citrusy, with a woody/spicy bitterness"; and Chinook, a high-alpha hop he uses for bittering in his Barleywine and Red. His use of Willamette is on the decline because, he says, "I've become bored with it." John uses pellets for all his additions, even dry hopping. With the acquisition of a new hopback, he hopes to start experimenting with some leaf hops.

When choosing hops, research the pedigree of the hop. Learn what the variety was derived from to determine how it should best be used in brewing. You should always know the alpha acid level of your hops. High-alpha hops (7–10 percent) have their place as bittering hops, and in stronger, high-gravity beers, but low-alpha hops (3–5 percent) will give more hop flavor and aroma when added late. A low percentage of co-humulone will contribute to a dense head. When calculating International Bitterness Units for a recipe, John's approach is more intuitive than scientific, and he usually errs on the high side.

John boils his wort for 90 minutes, and most of his beers have additions at the start of the boil, at 60 minutes, and then a final addition after the boil, in the whirlpool. With his latest batch of Mogul, John has been experimenting with what he calls first wort hopping. Hop pellets are added to the kettle at the start of the run-off from the mash tun. This addition essentially steeps for 2 hours before the boil commences. "It creates a finer, more refined bitterness than you get from a boiling hop," John says. Oddly enough, he also claims it improves aroma characteristics even though the hops are subsequently boiled for 90 minutes.

At the 1996 Great American Beer Festival, the three award-winning recipes in the Smoked Beer Category were, in some way or other, attributable to John Maier. John warns against the temptation of using liquid smoke to produce these styles. It is much more authentic, and quite easy, to smoke your own malt.

Rogue Smoke, the GABF medal winner seven times, is made with Northwest Harrington and Klages, Crystal, Carastan, and Bamberg Beechwood smoked pale malt, which has a delicate aroma. Finally, John hand-smokes about 50 pounds of Munich malt in a backyard smoker for a rich flavor and aroma. This perennial favorite is reportedly derived from John's original 5-gallon recipe.

The best way to smoke malt for your homebrew is to take about 1/2 to 1 pound of your base or specialty malt, crack, and wet it with a sprinkle of water. Spread the malt evenly on a window screen, and place the window screen on a charcoal barbecue, prepared with a decent-smoking wood. John prefers alder for its rich smoke; beechwood produces a drier flavor, and cherry is nice too. When the wood is smoldering well—*not* burning—and producing a steady stream of smoke, place the malt in the barbecue and cover for about 30 minutes. Check for doneness by holding a handful of the grain about 6 inches from your nose; the intensity of the aroma will give you a good indication of the intensity of flavor to expect.

*The following recipes were taken from Zymurgy Special Issue 1988 with permission from John Maier. The recipes are for 5-gallon batches.*

# HUMPBACK LAGER

**1988 American Homebrewer's Association National Homebrew Competition: First Place, Vienna Category**

6 POUNDS PALE KLAGES MALT

3 POUNDS MUNICH MALT

3/4 POUND CARA-PILS MALT

1/2 POUND CRYSTAL MALT, 40 DEGREES LOVIBOND

1 OUNCE HALLERTAUER HOPS

1/2 OUNCE HALLERTAUER HOPS

1/2 OUNCE HALLERTAUER HOPS

1/4 TEASPOON YEASTEX

1 PACKAGE WYEAST AMERICAN LAGER LIQUID YEAST

3/4 CUP DEXTROSE TO PRIME

OG: 1.052 • TG: 1.012

Mash all grains at 120°F for 30 minutes. Infuse boiling water to raise the temperature to 153°F for 15 minutes. Apply heat, and raise the temperature to 170°F. Sparge with 170°F water. Collect 6 gallons sweet wort. Boil for 90 minutes, adding 1 ounce Hallertauer hops after 30 minutes and 1/2 ounce Hallertauer hops after 80 minutes. Turn off heat and add 1/2 ounce Hallertauer hops, and steep for 15 minutes. Cool wort, and pitch yeast and yeast nutrient. Ferment and lager to terminal gravity. Bottle using dextrose.

## OREGON SPECIAL

1988 Homebrewer of the Year, First Place,
Barleywine Category

---

11 POUNDS WILLIAMS AUSTRALIAN DRY MALT EXTRACT
3 POUNDS KLAGES MALT
5 OUNCES NUGGET HOPS
1 1/2 OUNCES WILLAMETTE HOPS
8 OUNCES YEAST STARTER OF SIERRA NEVADA CULTURE
3/4 CUP DEXTROSE TO PRIME

OG: 1.075 • FG: 1.025

Mash grains at 120°F for 30 minutes. Raise heat to 130°F. Infuse boiling water, and raise to 152°F for 15 minutes. Raise heat to 158°F for 10 minutes. Raise to 170°F. Sparge with 2 gallons of 170°F water. Boil for 90 minutes, adding 5 ounces Nugget hops after 45 minutes and 1 1/2 ounces Willamette hops after 80 minutes. Cool wort and pitch yeast. Ferment to final gravity and condition. Bottle using dextrose.

## 14.

# RAY MCNEILL

## *McNeill's Pub and Brewery*

*[On the difference between open and closed fermentation:] "Who cares!? The yeast doesn't know! It doesn't have any eyes! The yeast doesn't know whether there's a lid on it or not!"*

**T**echnically, Ray McNeill was never a homebrewer. He never brewed in his home ("because I didn't have one"), but he did put together a homebrew-scale system for his pub in Vermont on which he brewed some outstanding beers, and built his reputation as one of New England's foremost craft brewers.

Ray is owner and brewer at McNeill's Pub in Brattleboro, Vermont. When he was looking for a way to differentiate his bar from the others in the area, he noted the burgeoning craft beer industry and thought brewing might be the answer. Rather than take the path most of us are familiar with—buying a homebrew kit and following the instructions—Ray consulted technical literature to understand the direction he was to take his business. Ray devoured *The Practical Brewer, Malting and Brewing Science (Vols. 1 and 2), Principles of Brewing Science,* and *Modern Brewing Technology.* "When I finished *The Practical Brewer* the first time, I understood about 15 percent of it," says Ray. Committing a year of his life as an unpaid apprentice for Catamount Brewery in White River

Junction, Vermont, Ray gleaned all the information he could on the brewing process. He read through his brewing texts two more times before opening McNeill's in 1990.

While many brewers rely heavily on experience, Ray backs up his hands-on experience with encyclopedic textbook knowledge. For Ray, it is essential to research and think through every aspect of the brewing process. When choosing the right ingredients, he is a slave to style. Knowing grains and the flavor profile they will produce is very important. A brewer shouldn't stop at simply choosing a British malt for a British-style beer; rather, he or she should be creative and use a variety of malts to employ the best characteristics of each. Ray recommends blending pale malts to overcome minor shortcomings in one basic variety. For instance, Ray uses nearly 100 percent Maris Otter pale malt in his Duck's Breath Bitter, but there are two problems with Maris Otter according to Ray: "One is that it's very mealy and has a coarse, almost malt-derived bitterness, which I think is appropriate for a bitter or India pale ale but may be a bad selection for an English brown or stout. Also, the diastatic power of the malt is incredibly low, and we get poor attenuation when we use 100 percent, so we blend in some domestic Harrington two-row klages."

Ray is emphatic about the use of two-row malt. The smaller kernels of six-row malt contain less starch and more husk than two-row. They tend to produce a very phenolic beer with an astringent, nonhop bitterness. Ray thinks that the popularity of American six-row developed over 100 years ago because the grain grew better in the United States and brewers used what was available. By adding other fermentables, like corn and rice, they were able to make better beers. "They found out empirically that if they added some non-malt adjuncts, the flavor improved," Ray theorizes. Six-row malts are also higher in protein and free amino nitrogen. Excess levels of free amino nitrogen adversely affect flocculation, thus producing cloudier beers. Ray surmises, "The early brewers, not having filters, probably realized that their beers dropped brighter when they used adjuncts."

The two-row malt that is generally available today is well modified by the maltsters. This means that the starches are readily available for conversion to fermentable sugars and easily accessed by the brewer. Well-modified malts require only single-infusion mashing, perfect for basic ale production. Ray has experimented with decoction mashing and upward infusion, or step, mashing techniques over the years. Decoction can be a nightmare if the brewer is not properly equipped to move boiling mash around, but if you are, the method is great for lagers or even kolsch or alt. Ray sees little benefit gained from doing a double or triple decoction. "Double and triple decoctions are probably better, but single decoctions are very effective and relatively fast. It's really not worth the time and energy expended." The upward infusion method of mashing is "the best of both worlds." Heating the mash directly takes it through the temperature rests normally dictated by a decoction schedule, without the mess of transferring boiling mash around. But at the brewpub level, single infusion is the preferred mashing method. "If one were very large, the efficiency of the extract might improve if one were to get involved with upward infusion or temperature-programmed infusion. The economics only improve on a large scale."

As every brewer knows, textbook knowledge isn't always enough; ingredient selection is also strongly influenced by practical experience. Ray wanted to believe that whole-flower hops were superior, that they have a certain integrity. However, he now uses pellets for all hop additions because they are extremely practical. They are consistently fresher, easier to store, and easier to use than leaf hops. "When they are exceptionally fresh and well cared for, flower hops might have a slight advantage, but that's only under ideal circumstances." Pellet hops are also more advantageous when dry hopping. Whole-leaf hops tend to float and may not be utilized as effectively as pellets, which will become fully immersed.

Through experience and research, Ray has found that a long, hard boil is fundamental to brewing. Sixty minutes is too short for the boil to be truly effective. Ninety minutes is the minimum boil that Ray recommends, and 2 hours for a barleywine. A 90-minute boil is superior for the protein break it provides. A good, hard boil should evaporate between 8 and 12 percent of the wort. These evaporation rates are effective at driving off wort volatiles such as dimethyl sulfide, which contributes a creamed corn flavor to beer, "as well as parsnip, but who the hell knows what parsnip tastes like?" Ray reminds us, "The harder the boil, the better the beer—the cleaner the hot break, the finer the quality of the bitterness, the fewer the wort volatiles."

To improve your brewing skills, Ray's advice is to read voraciously. Books he suggests are *Principles of Brewing Science* by George Fix, *The Practical Brewer* (available from the Master Brewers Association of America), *Malting and Brewing Science* (vols. 1 and 2) by D. E. Briggs, J. S. Hough, R. Stevens, and T. W. Young, and *Textbook of Brewing Science* by Jean de Clerck.

# DOPPELBOCK

12 POUNDS, 9 OUNCES GERMAN PILSNER MALT

5 POUNDS, 5 OUNCES LIGHT MUNICH MALT

1 POUND, 4 OUNCES ENGLISH CRYSTAL MALT (APPROX. 60L)

4 OUNCES MALTED WHEAT

3 OUNCES CHOCOLATE MALT

1/2 OUNCE TETTNANGER HOPS, 4.6% ALPHA, KETTLE

2/3 OUNCE TETTNANGER HOPS, 4.6% ALPHA, 30 MIN.

1 OUNCE HALLERTAUER HOPS, 3.1% ALPHA, 30 MIN. (LIBERTY, CRYSTAL, OR LEAST OF ALL, MT. HOOD COULD BE SUBSTITUTED IF HALLERTAUER IS UNATTAINABLE)

1 PACKAGE WYEAST 2206 (AND 2308, OPTIONAL), ALONG WITH SOME MALT EXTRACT FOR GROWTH MEDIUM

Crush malt, retaining the Munich separately. Mash the remaining malts with 4 1/2 gallons water at 140°F and 1/4 ounce calcium carbonate ($CaCl_2$).

In a heavy stainless pot, mash the Munich malt with 0.8 ounce (or 2 grams) $CaCl_2$ and 2 1/2 gallons of water at 110°F. Raise the temperature gently to 151°F, stirring the bottom to ensure it's not sticking and burning. Rest 10 minutes at 150°F. Then bring to a boil. Boil the mash for 10 minutes, then return to the main mash, stirring thoroughly. The main mash should have rested a sufficient amount of time while the decoction was performed for adequate saccharification.

Sparge with enough water to achieve 5 gallons at the end of the boil (difficult to predict based on unknown evaporation) and 1/6 ounce (or 5 grams) $CaCl_2$. Bring wort to a boil and add 1/2 ounce Tettnanger hops. Boil for 90 minutes, adding 2/3 ounce Tettnanger hops and Hallertauer hops after 30 minutes. Cool to 45°F.

Pitch Wyeast 2206 propagated according to the instructions, or the same yeast in "monster bag" size. Ferment at 53°F. After fermentation (about 12 days), allow to warm to 58°F for 1 day (diacetyl rest) before cooling to 38°F. Hold at 38°F for 1 month. If you have carbon dioxide, drop a sanitized hose into the bottom of the carboy a couple of days before transfer and slowly bubble some carbon dioxide into the bottom for 10 or 20 minutes. Allow to drop bright again.

This beer could now be primed and bottled, but it will take a year to taste right. It could be force-carbonated in a keg and (you will be) drunk in a week.

To make a really nice beer, mix up 1/2 gallon of hopped (extract) wort or brew a conventional gravity all-grain Vienna lager (preferred) or pilsner, about 12 Plato (1.048). Either way, inoculate 1/2 gallon with Wyeast 2308, and mix with Dopplebock the next day and bottle (or keg, if you must. You've gone to so much trouble, why not go the extra mile?). Hold this at 38°F for at least 3 months and you will win a medal.

# AUTHORS' RECIPES

Here are 40 new recipes of our own. Some are our favorites that didn't make it into *The Homebrewer's Recipe Guide*, and others are new ones that were inspired by our interviews with the great brewers we met while doing this book.

All of the following recipes yield 5 gallons.

## BAVARIAN MÄRZEN

This one tries to live up to Michael Ferguson's exacting standards. It is true to style, requiring decoction and a lengthy and precise lagering period. Munich malt and noble hops are essential ingredients. Reinheitsgebot forbids the use of corn sugar or other adjuncts, so stick to malt extract if bottling, or krausen.

7 POUNDS PALE 2-ROW MALT

1 1/2 POUNDS MUNICH MALT

1 1/2 POUNDS CARASTAN MALT

3/4 OUNCE TETTNANGER HOPS

1/2 OUNCE NORTHERN BREWER HOPS

1/2 OUNCE TETTNANGER HOPS

1 TEASPOON IRISH MOSS
WYEAST 2468 OR 2068 LAGER YEAST
1 CUP DRIED MALT EXTRACT (IF NOT FORCE CARBONATING)

OG: 1.047

**M**ash in at 152°F for 30 minutes. Scoop out one-fourth of the mash, and boil for 15 minutes, adding water if the mixture seems dry. Remix into the mash, mashing out at 168°F. Sparge and collect wort. Bring to a boil and add 3/4 ounce Tettnanger hops and Northern Brewer hops. Boil for 90 minutes, adding 1/2 ounce Tettnanger hops and Irish moss for the final 5 minutes. Cool wort to 40°F and pitch yeast. Let the temperature rise to 48–51°F for 5 days. Transfer to a secondary fermenter, and ferment an additional 3 to 4 days. Lower the temperature (as slowly as possible) back down to 32°F for lagering. Lager for 4 to 6 weeks. Bottle or keg. Age 7 to 10 days before serving.

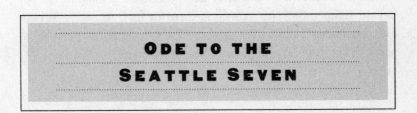

# ODE TO THE
# SEATTLE SEVEN

**S**ince its opening in 1992, Pike Place has been a leader in the Seattle beer world. One notable example is the brewery's reputation for training great brewers. In fact, seven of Pike's assistant brewers have moved on to head brewer positions in Seattle and beyond. This recipe was inspired by the elements of Seattle's signature style: a proliferation of Chinook and Cascade, balanced by a medium-bodied, full-flavored ale. No doubt these seven have had a lot to do with creating this signature Northwest style.

7 POUNDS PALE 2-ROW MALT

1 POUND MUNICH MALT

2 POUNDS CRYSTAL MALT (60L)

2 OUNCES CHINOOK HOPS

1 OUNCE CASCADE HOPS

2 OUNCES CASCADE HOPS

2 OUNCES CASCADE HOPS

2 TEASPOONS GYPSUM

1 TEASPOON IRISH MOSS

AMERICAN ALE YEAST 1056

3/4 CUP CORN SUGAR

OG: 1.048

Combine malts and mash for 1 hour at 155°F. Sprinkle gypsum over the top of the mash, sparge, and collect wort. Bring to a boil. Add Chinook hops. Boil for 45 minutes, adding 1 ounce Cascade hops. Boil for another 45 minutes, adding 2 ounces Cascade hops and Irish moss for the final 5 minutes. Cool wort to 62°F and pitch yeast. Let the temperature rise to 66°F, fermenting for 5 to 7 days. When fully attenuated, allow for a diacetyl rest. Drop the temperature if you plan to harvest the yeast. Then transfer to a secondary fermenter, add the final 2 ounces Cascade hops, and allow to condition for 3 to 5 days. Bottle, using corn sugar, or keg.

# NAKED MAN STOUT

**T**here are two small islands located in a mountain lake in California's Yosemite National Park. They were discovered by two adventuresome beer lovers when, after a long afternoon of hiking, they came upon the most picturesque spot any brewer has ever seen. After setting up camp, they fearlessly plunged into the lake and set out for the islands. Near-freezing water temperatures threatened to turn them back to camp, but they prevailed. Blue and shivering on the shores of their discovery, they howled in triumph and dubbed the islands the Naked Man Islands. After much procrastination, the brewers returned to camp and broke out the stout they had packed in to warm them by the fire. While the exact location of the islands shall remain a secret, we will share the stout recipe with you.

9 POUNDS PALE MALT

1 POUND CRYSTAL MALT (DARK)

1/2 POUND KARAFFE CHOCOLATE MALT

1/2 POUND ROASTED BARLEY

1 POUND LACTOSE

1 TEASPOON GYPSUM

1 1/2 OUNCES EAST KENT GOLDINGS HOPS, 4.5% ALPHA

1/2 OUNCE EAST KENT GOLDINGS HOPS, 4.5% ALPHA

2 PACKAGES DANSTAR NOTTINGHAM YEAST

1 CUP CORN SUGAR (PRIMING)

OG: 1.070 • FG: 1.018

**M**ash grains with 130°F water and gypsum for 30 minutes. Add enough boiling water over 20 minutes to achieve a temperature of 150–155°F. Sparge out with 170°F water. Run off 6 gallons. Boil for

90 minutes. Add bittering hops at the start of the boil and flavoring hops for the final 15 minutes. Cool wort to 70°F and pitch yeast starter. Ferment at 68–70°F for 10 days. Boil priming sugar in 1 quart of water for 5 minutes. Cool and mix with fermented wort in bottling bucket. Bottle condition for 7 days.

## IMPERIAL NORTHWEST

Imperial stouts, with their overwhelming malt and, especially, hop character, are truly magnificent beers. This one is brewed in the Northwest style. Granted, it's not a very long journey from the Northwest across the Bering Strait to Russia, so you really don't need all those hops for a preservative. Wait a second, what are we saying! Of course, you need them!

17 POUNDS PALE 2-ROW MALT

1 POUND MUNICH MALT

2 POUNDS CRYSTAL MALT (120L)

1 3/4 POUNDS ROASTED BARLEY

4 OUNCES CHINOOK HOPS

3 OUNCES CHINOOK HOPS

4 OUNCES CHINOOK HOPS, WHOLE LEAF

WYEAST 1056 ALE YEAST

OG: 1.100

Mash grain at 152–155°F for 60 minutes. Sparge and collect wort. Bring wort to a boil, and add 4 ounces Chinook hops. Boil for 90 minutes, adding 3 ounces Chinook hops during the final 5 minutes. As wort comes to a boil, place 4 ounces whole-leaf Chinook hops in hop tea chamber and fill with 160°F water. Set aside. When boil is complete, drain hop tea into a separate vessel, and then siphon hot wort through hops in the hop tea chamber. Cool wort and pitch yeast. Ferment for 7 to 10 days. Transfer to a secondary fermenter, and ferment an additional 14 to 21 days. Bottle or keg. Age 6 to 8 months before serving.

# XXX ALE

In March 1997, we received a letter from Michael Martin, a homebrewer who had purchased *The Homebrewer's Recipe Guide*. In the letter he shared a story with us of a particular steak house in Dallas that he would visit while home on leave from Vietnam. It was at this steak house that he fell in love with a girl (whom he's still married to) and a beer—Ballantine XXX Golden Ale, which he is no longer able to get in Texas.

He asked if we could help him out and supply him with a recipe. Unfortunately at the time, we couldn't. None of us had tasted Ballantine, or if we had, we'd forgotten. Then one evening in August 1997, as Patrick and two friends (both professional brewers) were buying beer in preparation for an evening of televised wrestling, they came across a bottle of Ballantine XXX Golden for 99 cents. Remembering the letter, Patrick bought some. To all of their surprise, they found it a fine American ale with some real malt and hop flavor. Thus began the journey to create a recipe for Mr. Martin.

After much Ballantine and much discussion, a recipe was created, except for the right yeast, which all brewers know is the key. Then fate stepped in. In our interview with Ray McNeill, he mentioned how fond he was of the Sierra Nevada yeast or Wyeast 1056. "I wondered where they got the yeast, only to find out it was Ballantine Ale yeast," Ray said. The recipe was complete, and here it is. Sorry for the long story, but we thought it was a good one.

6 3/4 POUNDS AMERICAN 2-ROW KLAGES MALT

1/4 POUND MUNICH MALT (20L)

3/4 POUND RICE, COOKED

3/4 POUND FLAKED MAIZE

1 1/4 OUNCES CRYSTAL MALT (20L)

2 OUNCES WILLAMETTE HOPS, 4.5% ALPHA

2 OUNCES WILLAMETTE HOPS, 4.5% ALPHA

WYEAST 1056 (AMERICAN ALE YEAST)

2 TEASPOONS IRISH MOSS

3/4 CUP CORN SUGAR (IF NOT FORCE-CARBONATING)

OG: 1.047

Mash grains for 30 minutes at 135°F. Raise the mash temperature to 160°F and mash an additional 30 minutes. Sparge and collect wort. Bring wort to a boil, and add 2 ounces Willamette hops. Boil for 60 minutes, adding 2 ounces Willamette hops for the final 5 minutes. Cool wort and pitch yeast. Ferment for 5 to 7 days. Transfer to a secondary fermenter, and ferment an additional 3 to 5 days. Drop the temperature to 40°F and condition an additional 2 days. Bottle or keg. Age for 5 to 7 days before serving.

# CARRY YOUR OWN

**T**he touch of black malt presses this brown ale toward the porter style. Many who tried this beer felt it was "too weak" to be a porter—hence the name. As a brown ale, it is almost bittersweet, like baker's chocolate. If you prefer a more traditional English brown, do away with the black patent.

7 1/2 POUNDS BRITISH 2-ROW PALE MALT

1/2 POUND CHOCOLATE MALT

1/4 POUND BLACK PATENT MALT

2 GRAMS GYPSUM

1 OUNCE EAST KENT GOLDINGS HOPS, 4.5% ALPHA (BITTERING)

1/4 OUNCE EAST KENT GOLDINGS HOPS, 4.5% ALPHA (FLAVORING)

1 PACKAGE IRISH ALE YEAST (WYEAST 1084)

3/4 CUP CORN SUGAR (PRIMING)

## OG: 1.043

**M**ash grains and gypsum at 150°F for 90 minutes. Run off 6 gallons of wort, or until gravity reaches 1.007, whichever comes first. Boil for 60 minutes. Add bittering hops at the start of the boil and flavoring hops for the final 15 minutes. Cool wort to 70°F and pitch yeast starter. Ferment at 68–70°F for 7 days. Rack to a secondary fermenter, and condition for a further 7 days. Bottle with corn sugar and condition for at least 7 days.

# BROWN AND MILD EYES

I entered the pub, leaving the bustle of the bright afternoon behind. The low ceiling and heavily dressed windows made the room seem almost earthen, cavelike, comfortable. My eyes slowly adjusted to the dark as I looked around at the few men and one woman seated at the four stained wooden tables. I approached the bar and sat alone at the near end. Fidgeting with a pile of coasters lying there, I scanned the rank of tap handles, wondering which would suit my mood. After a few moments, the barmaid approached and looked at me with brown and mild eyes. I knew what I wanted.

6 POUNDS BRITISH 2-ROW PALE MALT

1/2 POUND HUGH BAIRD BROWN MALT

1 TEASPOON GYPSUM

3/4 OUNCE FUGGLES HOPS, 5% ALPHA (BITTERING)

1/2 OUNCE FUGGLES HOPS, 5% ALPHA (FLAVORING)

1 PACKAGE LONDON ALE YEAST (WYEAST 1028)

2/3 CUP BROWN SUGAR (PRIMING)

OG: 1.038

Mash grains and gypsum at 148°F for 90 minutes. Collect 6 gallons of wort in a brew kettle. Boil for 90 minutes. Add bittering hops for the final 45 minutes of boil and flavoring hops for the final 30 minutes. Cool wort to 70°F and pitch yeast starter. Ferment at 68–70°F for 7 days. Rack to a secondary fermenter and condition for a further 7 days. Bottle with brown sugar and condition for at least 7 days.

# MOONBEAM'S BEST BITTER

Moonbeam's favorite style is best bitter, and this recipe is for this special friend of Paul's. Lava lamps, tie-dye, and the Grateful Dead are not listed in the ingredients below, but it can't hurt to include them. The water treatment and Maris Otter pale malt give this beer a distinct British accent, but the Dead would make it an authentic Moonbeam.

7 POUNDS MARIS OTTER PALE MALT

1/2 POUND CRYSTAL MALT (20L)

3 GRAMS GYPSUM

1 GRAM EPSOM SALTS

1 1/2 OUNCES NORTHERN BREWER HOPS,
7% ALPHA (BITTERING)

1/2 OUNCE PROGRESS HOPS, 5% ALPHA (FLAVORING)

1 PACKAGE BRITISH ALE YEAST (WYEAST 1098)

3/4 CUP CORN SUGAR (PRIMING)

## OG: 1.043

Mash grains and gypsum at 148–150°F (add Epsom salts to the mash water) for 90 minutes. Collect 6 gallons of wort in a brew kettle. Boil for 60 minutes, adding bittering hops at the start of the boil and flavoring hops for the final 15 minutes. Cool wort to 65°F and pitch yeast starter. Ferment at 65–68°F for 7 days. Rack to a secondary fermenter, and condition for a further 7 days. Bottle with corn sugar and condition for at least 7 days.

# MÄRZEN MALAISE

**T**he American pale malt in this recipe was used for the convenience of a single-infusion mash. A better alternative would be to use a well-modified lager malt and step the mash up from a protein-saccharification rest at 130°F to 155°F after the first 15 minutes. Better still, try decocting a European lager malt.

9 POUNDS AMERICAN 2-ROW PALE MALT
1/2 POUND MUNICH MALT
1/4 POUND CARA-PILS MALT
1 OUNCE TETTNANGER HOPS, 4.2% ALPHA (BITTERING)
1 OUNCE SPALT HOPS, 3.4% ALPHA (FLAVOR/AROMA)
1 PACKAGE MUNICH LAGER YEAST (WYEAST 2308)

OG: 1.052

**M**ash grains at 154°F for 90 minutes. Collect 6 gallons of wort in a brew kettle, and boil for 90 minutes. Add bittering hops for the final 60 minutes of the boil and flavoring hops for the final 10 minutes. Cool wort to 55°F and pitch yeast starter. Ferment at 50–55°F for 14 days. Rack to a secondary fermenter, and condition at 45°F for a further 2 months.

# SCHMOKE BIER

**T**his lager is an attempt to meld the characteristics of a German schwarzbier with those of the rauchbier. The beechwood imparts a dry smokiness that accentuates the bitterness of the black malt, but without overpowering the beer. Smoke aroma and flavor are subtle. For a smokier flavor, use Beechwood smoked pale malt, available from Weyermann Malts.

8 POUNDS GERMAN PALE LAGER MALT

1/2 POUND CHOCOLATE MALT

1/4 POUND BLACK PATENT MALT

1/2 POUND CRYSTAL MALT

1 1/4 OUNCES HALLERTAUER HOPS, 3.5% ALPHA (BITTERING)

1/2 OUNCE TETTNANGER HOPS, 4.2% ALPHA (FLAVOR/AROMA)

1 PACKAGE PILSNER LAGER YEAST (WYEAST 2007)

OG: 1.048

**C**rush 1 pound of the pale malt and spread evenly on a piece of window screen. Smoke over smoldering beechwood in a barbecue or smoker. (Refer to chapter 13 if necessary.) Mash grains with about 3 gallons of water to achieve a rest temperature of 130–135°F. After 15 minutes, decoct one-third of the mash, bringing it slowly to a boil over 20 to 25 minutes. Boil for 5 minutes and return it to the main mash, mixing thoroughly to attain a saccharification temperature of 152–155°F. Hold the temperature for 30 to 60 minutes. Add boiling water to increase the mash temperature to 170°F. Sparge with 170°F water. Collect 6 gallons of wort and boil 90 minutes. Add bittering hops for the final 60 minutes of the boil, and flavoring hops for the final 20 minutes. Cool wort and pitch starter when the temperature reaches 50°F. Ferment at 45–50°F until attenuated. Lager 2 months at 45°F.

# CALIFORNIA CREAMER

**C**ream ale is created by blending top-fermented wort with bottom-fermented wort. This single-fermentation cream ale approximates this blend by using a lager yeast at ale temperatures, much like the California Common, or Steam Beer.

7 1/2 POUNDS AMERICAN TWO-ROW PALE MALT

1 POUND MALTED WHEAT

1/4 OUNCE MT. HOOD HOPS, 5.5%

1/2 OUNCE MT. HOOD HOPS, 5.5%

1/4 OUNCE CASCADE HOPS, 6.0%

1 PACKAGE CALIFORNIA LAGER YEAST (WYEAST 2112)

3/4 CUP CORN SUGAR (PRIMING)

OG: 1.050

**M**ash grains at 148–150°F for 90 minutes. Collect 6 gallons of wort in a brew kettle and boil for 90 minutes. Add 1/4 ounce Mt. Hood hops at the start of the boil and 1/2 ounce Mt. Hood hops for the final 60 minutes of the boil. Add the Cascade hops for the final 30 minutes. Cool wort to 60°F and pitch yeast starter. Ferment at 60–65°F until attenuated. Cold-condition at 50°F for 1 week and lager for 2 months at 40°F. Bottle using corn sugar.

# PINSEL MACHER PILSNER

**D**inkelsbühl is a small town in Bavaria. In an old schoolhouse on the outskirts of the town is a small paintbrush factory known as Hertlein Pinsel. This family business has steadily grown for over 30 years and is now known as the finest manufacturer of artist and makeup brushes in Europe. Each brush is painstakingly assembled by hand from the finest sable and squirrel hairs available. If you happen to be in the area, stop by and ask for Reiner Hertlein, or any of his three sons. Tell them cousin Paul says, "Prosit!"

6 1/2 POUNDS WELL-MODIFIED PALE LAGER MALT

1 POUND MUNICH MALT

1/2 POUND CARA-PILS MALT

3/4 OUNCE PERLE HOPS, 7.2%

3/4 OUNCE SPALT HOPS, 4.2%

1/2 OUNCE TETTNANGER HOPS, 4.5%

1 PACKAGE CZECH PILS YEAST (WYEAST 2278)

3/4 CUP CORN SUGAR (PRIMING)

OG: 1.047

**M**ash grains at 148–150°F for 90 minutes. Add Perle hops to the brew kettle as you start to run off the wort from the mash. Collect 6 gallons of wort in the brew kettle and boil for 90 minutes. Add Spalt hops for the final 45 minutes of the boil and Tettnanger hops at the completion of the boil. Steep for 15 minutes. Cool wort to 50°F and pitch yeast starter. Ferment at 50–55°F until attenuated. Lager for 2 months at 35–40°F. Bottle using corn sugar.

# BLACK BREAD STOUT

**Y**ou have often heard of beer referred to as liquid bread. Well, this is liquid rye bread, complete with caraway seeds. This dry stout uses flaked rye to create a crisp flavor. The caraway will create a tannic bite that is hard to pick out through the roasted flavors. Be sure not to overdo it.

7 POUNDS BRITISH PALE MALT

1 1/2 POUNDS FLAKED RYE

1/2 POUND CHOCOLATE MALT

1/2 POUND ROASTED BARLEY

1/2 POUND CRYSTAL MALT (50L)

2 GRAMS GYPSUM

1/2 OUNCE CENTENNIAL HOPS, 10.5% (BITTERING)

1/2 OUNCE PERLE HOPS, 7.0% (FLAVORING)

1 TEASPOON CARAWAY SEEDS

1 PACKAGE IRISH ALE YEAST (WYEAST 1084)

3/4 CUP CORN SUGAR (PRIMING)

OG: 1.042

**M**ash grains and gypsum at 148–150°F for 90 minutes. Slowly run off wort from the mash (flaked rye can cause a stuck mash). Carefully collect 6 gallons of wort in a brew kettle, and boil for 60 minutes. Add bittering hops at the start of the boil and flavoring hops for the final 30 minutes. Cool wort to 65°F and pitch a well-started yeast culture. Ferment at 65–68°F until attenuated. Rack to a secondary fermenter, and condition for a further 7 to 14 days. Add flavor by suspending 1 teaspoon of caraway seeds in the secondary fermenter, and taste the stout periodically to determine if the flavor is apparent. Bottle using corn sugar.

# "I BEG YOUR PARDON"

**A**lthough I do not consider my travels and beer knowledge to be extensive, I have sampled my share of microbrews. The finest example of porter I have yet tasted was at Sherlock's Home in Minnetonka, Minnesota. Bill Burdick has created the most British of experiences in the chilly Midwest, not to mention a singularly stunning bar-back. This porter is nothing like Bill's, and I beg your pardon if I have confused the issue.

8 POUNDS BRITISH PALE MALT

1 POUND BLACK PATENT MALT

1 POUND DARK MUNICH MALT (30L)

1/2 POUND CARA MUNICH

2 GRAMS GYPSUM

3/4 OUNCES NORTHERN BREWER HOPS, 8.2% (BITTERING)

1/2 OUNCE NORTHERN BREWER HOPS, 8.2% (FLAVORING)

1 PACKAGE LONDON ALE YEAST (WYEAST 1028)

3/4 CUP CORN SUGAR (PRIMING)

OG: 1.055

**M**ash grains and gypsum at 153–155°F for 90 minutes. Collect 6 gallons of wort in a brew kettle and boil for 90 minutes. Add bittering hops for the last 60 minutes of boil and flavoring hops for the final 20 minutes. Cool wort to 65°F and pitch a well-started yeast culture. Ferment at 70–72°F until attenuated. Rack to a secondary fermenter, and condition for a further 7 days. Bottle using corn sugar.

# POPEYE IN A CAN

**N**o, this is not a spinach beer! This extract-based beer will knock your socks off. Lay these down for a while before laying them on your friends, or they may just sock you one. Extended aging, up to 1 year or more, will mellow this brew to the point where it is smooth as Olive Oyl.

4 KILOGRAMS EXTRA PALE MALT EXTRACT SYRUP

1 POUND GAMBRINUS HONEY MALT

1/2 POUND CARAMALT

1/4 POUND CHOCOLATE MALT

1 OUNCE NORTHERN BREWER HOPS, 8.2% (BITTERING)

3/4 OUNCE UK GOLDINGS HOPS, 4.2% (FLAVORING)

1/2 OUNCE FUGGLES HOPS, 3.2% (AROMA)

1 PACKAGE BRITISH ALE YEAST (WYEAST 1098)

3/4 CUP CORN SUGAR (PRIMING)

OG: 1.065

**S**teep cracked grains in 1 gallon of 155°F water for 15 minutes. Remove the brew kettle from the heat, and add malt extract, stirring constantly to prevent any scorching or caramelization. Add enough water to make 6 gallons of wort in the brew kettle. Heat to a boil, stirring constantly. Boil for 90 minutes. Add bittering hops for the last 60 minutes of boil and flavoring hops for the final 30 minutes. Steep the aroma hops for 15 minutes after completion of the boil. Cool wort to 65°F and pitch a well-started yeast culture. Ferment at 70–72°F until attenuated. Rack to a secondary fermenter, and condition for a further 14 days. Bottle with corn sugar and lay down for at least 3 months.

# OLD BLACK JOE

**W**hy is this recipe called Old Black Joe, especially when it's a pale fruit beer? Well, if you can guess, you could win a prize!! Welcome to the *Secrets from the Master Brewers Guess the Meaning of the Weird Recipe Name Contest*. Send your guesses to us, in care of Dan Lane at Fireside Books, 1230 Sixth Avenue, New York, NY 10020. The winner will receive one dented can of malt extract missing its label. Good luck!!!!!

5 POUNDS PALE 2-ROW MALT

3 POUNDS WHEAT MALT

1/2 POUND DEXTRINE MALT

1/2 POUND FLAKED BARLEY

1/2 POUND FLAKED WHEAT

1 OUNCE CASCADE HOPS

1/2 OUNCE LIBERTY HOPS

8 POUNDS PEACHES, PITTED, PEELED, SLICED (RETAIN THE PEEL OF 3 PEACHES)

WYEAST 3056 BAVARIAN WHEAT YEAST

## OG: 1.045

**M**ash grains for 60 minutes at 152°F. Sparge and collect wort. Bring to a boil and add Cascade hops. Boil for 90 minutes, adding Liberty hops for the final 5 minutes. Cool wort and pitch yeast. Ferment at 68°F for 5 to 7 days. Transfer to a secondary fermenter, add the peaches, and cool to 55°F. Condition for 3 to 5 days, add the peach peels on the last day. Bottle or keg. Age 5 to 7 days before serving.

# LIGHTHOUSE GOLDEN ALE

**T**his recipe and the next three were inspired by the Outer Banks of North Carolina, which is our favorite place on the planet. Every time we visit, we brew up plenty of homebrew for our stay. These are four of our favorites.

6 1/2 POUNDS PALE 2-ROW MALT

3/4 POUND FLAKED WHEAT

1 POUND FLAKED MAIZE

2 OUNCES IRISH MOSS

1 OUNCE CASCADE HOPS, 5%

1/2 OUNCE TETTNANGER HOPS, 4%

2 OUNCES CASCADE HOPS, 5%

AMERICAN ALE YEAST

3/4 CUP CORN SUGAR (IF NOT FORCE CARBONATING)

OG: 1.038

**M**ash grains at 155 degrees for 60–90 minutes. Collect wort and bring to a boil, adding 1 ounce Cascade hops. Boil for 90 minutes, adding 1/2 ounce Tettnanger hops after 45 minutes. Add Irish moss during the final 5 minutes of the boil. Remove from the heat. Place 2 ounces Cascade hops in a hop tea chamber, and fill with 170°F water. Drain hop tea into a secondary vessel, and then run the hot wort through the hop tea chamber. Cool wort and pitch yeast. Ferment at 68–72°F for 3 to 4 days. Transfer to a secondary fermenter and cool to 55°F. Ferment an additional 7 to 10 days. Bottle, using corn sugar, or keg. Age 7 to 10 days before serving.

# PEA ISLAND PALE ALE

**T**he savage coastline of the Outer Banks has claimed hundreds of ships and passenger lives throughout the years—so many that the coastline of the Outer Banks has become known as the "graveyard of the Atlantic." Prior to the formation of the U.S. Coast Guard, lifesaving stations were scattered up and down the beach. The one at Pea Island was unique in that its lifesaving record was superior to all other stations, but truly unique in that it was the only station manned by an all-African-American crew. Richard Etheridge and his crew became known as the best prepared and most dedicated of all the lifesavers who manned the stations. This beer is a tribute to them.

8 POUNDS PALE 2-ROW MALT

I POUND CRYSTAL MALT (80L)

I POUND WHEAT MALT

I OUNCE ROASTED BARLEY

2 TEASPOONS IRISH MOSS

2 OUNCES CHALLENGER HOPS, 7%

I OUNCE LIBERTY HOPS, 4%

I 1/2 OUNCES CASCADE HOPS

3/4 CUP CORN SUGAR (IF NOT FORCE CARBONATING)

WYEAST 1056 AMERICAN ALE YEAST

OG: 1.048

**M**ash grains at 155 degrees for 60 to 90 minutes. Collect wort and bring to a boil, adding Challenger hops. Boil for 90 minutes, adding 1/2 ounce Liberty hops after 45 minutes and 1/2 ounce after 60 minutes. Add Irish moss during the final 5 minutes of the boil.

Remove from the heat and add 1 1/2 ounces Cascade hops. Let sit for 15 minutes. Cool wort and pitch yeast. Ferment at 68–72°F for 3 to 5 days. Cool to 55°F and ferment an additional 7 to 10 days. Bottle, using corn sugar, or keg. Age 7 to 10 days before serving.

## KITTY HAWK WHEAT

**K**itty Hawk, North Carolina, is best known as the town where the Wright brothers made their first flight. But in reality, the Wright brothers' first flight took place 5 miles south in the town of Kill Devil Hills. So what does this have to do with this recipe? Nothing, really. So quit reading and go brew this beer.

4 1/2 POUNDS PALE 2-ROW MALT

3 1/2 POUNDS WHEAT MALT

1 POUND ROLLED OATS

1 1/2 OUNCES SAAZ HOPS, 3%

1/2 OUNCE SAAZ HOPS

WYEAST 3944 BELGIAN WHITE YEAST

OG: 1.040

**M**ash grains at 155 degrees for 60 to 90 minutes. Collect wort and bring to a boil, adding 1 1/2 ounces of Saaz hops. Boil for 90 minutes, adding 1/2 ounce Saaz hops after 80 minutes. Cool wort and pitch yeast. Ferment at 68–72 degrees for 2 to 4 days. Transfer to a secondary fermenter, and cool to 55°F. Ferment an additional 10 to 14 days. Bottle or keg. Age 7 to 10 days before serving.

# PAMLICO PORTER

**P**amlico Sound lies between the mainland and the southern islands of the Outer Banks. In its waters swim some of the most magnificent fish on the Atlantic Coast—namely bluefish, big bluefish. This porter is the perfect complement to a bluefish dinner. Its strong flavors hold up well to the dense, oily flavor of bluefish, or any other assertive fish like Spanish mackerel.

8 POUNDS PALE 2-ROW MALT

1 POUND WHEAT MALT

1 1/4 POUNDS CHOCOLATE MALT

1/8 POUND ROASTED BARLEY

1 OUNCE PERLE HOPS, 6%

1 OUNCE EAST KENT GOLDINGS HOPS, 5%

1 OUNCE EAST KENT GOLDINGS HOPS, 5%

WYEAST 1056 AMERICAN ALE YEAST

3/4 CUP CORN SUGAR (IF NOT FORCE CARBONATING)

OG: 1.054

**M**ash grains for 60 to 90 minutes. Collect wort and bring to a boil, adding Perle hops. Boil for 90 minutes, adding 1 ounce East Kent Goldings hops after 50 minutes and 1 ounce East Kent Goldings hops after 80 minutes. Cool wort and pitch yeast. Ferment at 68–72°F for 3 to 5 days. Transfer to a secondary fermenter, and cool to 55°F. Ferment an additional 7 to 10 days. Bottle, using corn sugar, or keg. Age 7 to 10 days before serving.

# WILD THING

**A**s we were doing the interviews for this book and asking questions about adjuncts, especially rice, both Dick Cantwell and Fal Allen mentioned a wild rice beer brewed by a former colleague at Pike. All of us thought it sounded like an adventurous and delicious beer. Here is our version.

7 POUNDS PALE 2-ROW MALT

2 POUNDS WILD RICE

1/2 POUND TORREFIED WHEAT

1/2 POUND MUNICH MALT

2 OUNCES CHINOOK HOPS

2 OUNCES CASCADE HOPS

AMERICAN ALE YEAST

OG: 1.045

**C**ook wild rice per package directions for 20 minutes, and let cool, retaining all liquid. Mash grains, including the wild rice, for 60 to 90 minutes. Collect wort and bring to a boil, adding Chinook hops. Boil for 90 minutes, adding Cascade hops during the final 10 minutes. Cool wort and pitch yeast. Ferment at 68–72°F for 7 to 10 days. Cool to 50°F and ferment an additional 3 to 4 days. Bottle or keg. Age 7 to 10 days before serving.

# NEW JUBILEE

This is based on cherries jubilee, a favorite recipe previously published in *The Homebrewer's Recipe Guide*. We've applied Jim Migliorini's tips for using fruit and oak flavorings to make a good thing even better. Note that we leave the cherry pits in this time for their added woody quality.

12 POUNDS PALE 2-ROW MALT

1 POUND CRYSTAL MALT (80L)

1/2 POUND FLAKED BARLEY

1/4 POUND CHOCOLATE MALT

2 POUNDS HONEY

2 OUNCES FUGGLES HOPS

1/2 OUNCE WILLAMETTE HOPS

12 POUNDS CHERRIES, CRUSHED; RETAIN PITS

2 CUPS OAK CHIPS

VODKA TO COVER WOOD CHIPS

1 PACKAGE ESB YEAST

OG: 1.073

Place the oak chips in a mason jar, and cover with vodka. Cover the jar and store it in the refrigerator for 1 week before brew day. Mash grains at 152°F for 90 minutes. Collect wort and bring to a boil, adding Fuggles hops and honey. Boil for 90 minutes, adding Willamette hops during the final 10 minutes. Cool wort and pitch yeast. Ferment at 68–72°F for 7 to 10 days. Transfer to a secondary fermenter. Cool to 50°F and add cherries and pits. Strain off vodka from the wood chips, and add the chips to the secondary fermenter. Ferment an additional 5 to 7 days. Strain, then bottle or keg. Age 10 to 14 days before serving.

# WHITE WEDDING

**F**or the wedding of a very dear friend, there is no gift as festive and personal as a hand-crafted beer. This one was created for Pam, who prefers wheat and rye beers. We varied our usual white beer accompaniments of curaçao orange and coriander with a subtle touch of lemon and clove. The honey contributes a translucent golden quality, which seems particularly appropriate for a wedding beer.

4 POUNDS PALE 2-ROW MALT

4 POUNDS MALTED WHEAT

1 POUND ROLLED OATS

1/4 POUND RYE MALT

1 POUND GOLDEN HONEY

1/2 OUNCE CHINOOK HOPS

PEEL OF 1/2 LEMON

4 CLOVES

BELGIAN WHITE YEAST

3/4 CUP CORN SUGAR

OG: 1.045

**S**teep grains for 30 minutes at 120°F. Raise the temperature to 135°F and hold for 20 minutes. Raise to the final mash temperature of 155°F for 20 minutes. Sparge and collect wort. Bring to a boil, add Chinook hops, and boil for 90 minutes. Cool wort and pitch yeast. Ferment at 68–70° for 5 to 7 days, until fully attenuated, allowing for a diacetyl rest. Drop the temperature if you plan to harvest yeast, and transfer to a secondary fermenter. Stud the lemon peel with the cloves, heat briefly in a microwave oven if possible, and add to the beer. Allow to condition 3 to 5 days, tasting for seasoning each day. Pull the lemon and cloves when the desired intensity is reached. Bottle, using the corn sugar, or keg.

# STAND UP DUBBEL

The warm character and subtle prune-raisin aroma of Belgian dubbels make them a wonderful complement to rich dishes like stews that warm up cold winter nights.

8 POUNDS BELGIAN 2-ROW MALT
1/2 POUND BELGIAN BISCUIT MALT
1/2 POUND BELGIAN SPECIAL B MALT
3 CUPS DARK CORN SYRUP
3/4 OUNCE PERLE HOPS, 7%
1/4 OUNCE PERLE HOPS, 7%
WYEAST 1214 BELGIAN ALE YEAST

OG: 1.058

Mash grain for 60 minutes at 152°F. Sparge and collect wort. Bring to a boil and add corn syrup and 3/4 ounce Perle hops. Boil for 90 minutes, adding 1/4 ounce Perle hops during the final 5 minutes. Cool wort and pitch yeast. Ferment at 70°F for 5 to 7 days. Transfer to a secondary fermenter, and condition an additional 7 to 10 days. Bottle or keg. Age 10 to 14 days before serving.

## MARY HAD A LITTLE LAMBIC

**F**or those of you who are relatively new to the craft beer boom, you may be a little intimidated by lambics. Not only is their brewing process a true enigma, but their flavor is a truly acquired taste. We're sure a few of you have cringed at your first taste, only to be berated by lambic lovers for your "crude" palate. Don't be bullied! These beers aren't for everyone. And if you find yourself berated by self-styled beer snobs, simply explain to them that you don't care for them but as a brewer you appreciate them. Then take the empty lambic bottle from the table, break it, and cut their eye out. (Just kidding.)

6 POUNDS BELGIAN 2-ROW MALT

4 POUNDS UNMALTED WHEAT

1 OUNCE SAAZ HOPS, 3%, OLD AND STALE

2 TABLESPOONS LACTIC ACID

WYEAST *Brettanomyces bruxellensis* YEAST

OG: 1.050

**M**ash grains for 60 minutes at 152°F. Sparge and collect wort. Boil for 90 minutes, adding the Saaz hops after 30 minutes. Cool wort and pitch yeast. When fermenting wort reaches 1.030, add lactic acid. Ferment for 5 to 7 days. Transfer to secondary fermenter, and condition for 12 weeks. Bottle or keg. Allow the beer to condition for 8 months to 1 year before serving.

# ONE-GRAIN STOUT

**A**n issue that many brewers disagreed on was whether to blend dark grains in beers like stouts and porters. One person who was adamant about this was Holy Cow's Dan Rogers, who insisted that no chocolate should be used in stouts and no roasted barley in porters. We came up with this recipe using Dan's mantra as our guide.

7 POUNDS PALE 2-ROW MALT

1 POUND MUNICH MALT

1 POUND FLAKED WHEAT

1 POUND CRYSTAL MALT (120L)

1 1/4 POUNDS ROASTED BARLEY

1 OUNCE CASCADE HOPS

1 OUNCE EAST KENT GOLDINGS HOPS

1 OUNCE EAST KENT GOLDINGS HOPS

1 1/2 OUNCES CASCADE HOPS (DRY HOP OR HOP TEA CHAMBER)

WYEAST 1056 AMERICAN ALE YEAST

OG: 1.052

**M**ash grains for 60 minutes at 156°F. Sparge and collect wort. Bring to a boil, and add 1 ounce Cascade hops and 1 ounce East Kent Goldings hops. Boil for 90 minutes, adding 1 ounce East Kent Goldings after 80 minutes. Run hot wort through the hop tea chamber, which contains 1 1/2 ounces Cascade hops. Cool wort and pitch yeast. Ferment at 68–72°F for 3 to 5 days. Transfer to a secondary fermenter, and cool to 55°F. Ferment an additional 7 to 10 days. Bottle or keg. Age 7 to 10 days before serving.

# BITE ME WHEAT

**T**his recipe was inspired by our interview with Fal Allen, who had brewed a heavily hopped wheat at Pike that found itself way out of style. Two customers who ordered it asked their server to tell the brewer that the beer was a terrible wheat—but a damn good pilsner. Regardless of the backhanded compliment, Fal was pleased. We decided to make our own version. Some of our beer snob friends have reacted the same way Fal's customers did: "This isn't a wheat! Do you know what you're doing?" To which we always respond, "Bite me."

4 POUNDS PALE 2-ROW MALT

4 POUNDS WHEAT MALT

1/4 POUND MUNICH MALT

2 OUNCES SAAZ HOPS

1 OUNCE SPALT HOPS

1 OUNCE SPALT HOPS

1/2 OUNCE SAAZ HOPS

WYEAST 3056 WHEAT YEAST

OG: 1.043

**M**ash grains at 155°F for 60–90 minutes. Collect wort and bring to a boil, adding 2 ounces Saaz hops and 1 ounce Spalt hops. Boil for 90 minutes, adding 1 ounce Spalt hops after 45 minutes. Remove from heat, and add 1/2 ounce Saaz hops. Let sit for 15 minutes. Cool wort and pitch yeast. Ferment at 65°F for 3 to 5 days. Cool to 55°F and ferment an additional 7 to 10 days. Cool to 40°F and ferment an additional 5 to 7 days. Bottle or keg. Age 7 to 10 days before serving.

# JENNIFER JUNIPER

**A**ttention gin lovers! The addition of juniper berries to this light ale gives it an interesting gin character in nose and flavor—and, if we may be so crude, in any belch, which will be an overwhelming gin character.

7 POUNDS PALE 2-ROW MALT

1 POUND TORREFIED WHEAT

1/4 POUND MUNICH MALT

1 OUNCE CHINOOK HOPS

1/2 OUNCE CASCADE HOPS

2 OUNCES JUNIPER BERRIES

WYEAST 1056 AMERICAN ALE YEAST

OG: 1.042

**M**ash grains for 60 minutes at 152°F. Sparge and collect wort. Bring to a boil and add Chinook hops and 1 ounce juniper berries. Remove from heat and add Cascade hops. Let rest for 5 minutes. Cool wort and pitch yeast. Ferment for 5 to 7 days. Transfer to a secondary fermenter, and add 1 ounce juniper berries. Condition for 4 to 5 days. Bottle or keg. Age for 5 to 7 days before serving.

# DESERT DUNKEL

**W**heat beers always seem especially quenching, so they are a popular choice in the desert town of Las Vegas. It is essential to use dark wheat here to provide color—not dark malts like chocolate or roasted barley. We like to toast our own wheat, fairly simple on a homebrew level. We also ferment at a slightly lower temperature, to get more vanilla and clove from the Weihenstephan yeast, rather than the banana esters we normally associate with a lighter wheat.

6 POUNDS PALE 2-ROW MALT

4 POUNDS UNMALTED WHEAT

I OUNCE PERLE HOPS

1/4 OUNCE SAAZ HOPS

WEIHENSTEPHAN YEAST

3/4 CUP CORN SUGAR

OG: 1.048

**T**oast wheat on cookie sheets in a preheated 425°F oven for 30 minutes. Cool slightly. Combine with the pale malt and mash for 1 hour at 155°F. Sparge and collect wort. Bring to a boil, add Perle hops, and boil for 90 minutes. Add Saaz hops at the end of the boil or use a hop back. Cool and transfer wort. Pitch yeast at 50°F. Let the temperature rise to 65°F and ferment 7 to 10 days. Transfer to a secondary fermenter, and cool to 50°F. Condition for 3 to 5 days. Bottle, using corn sugar, or keg. Age 5 to 7 days before serving.

# DAY TRIPPEL

While lighter in color than their dubbel neighbors, trippels are much stronger and higher in alcohol. These full-bodied beers should be savored, not chugged. If you have one, drink it in a brandy snifter glass to help capture the rich malt aroma.

11 POUNDS BELGIAN 2-ROW MALT

1/2 POUND BELGIAN CARA-PILS MALT

3 1/2 CUPS LIGHT CORN SYRUP

1 1/2 OUNCES SAAZ HOPS, 3%

1/2 OUNCE SAAZ HOPS, 3%

WYEAST 1214 BELGIAN ALE YEAST

1/4 CUP LIGHT CORN SYRUP (PRIMING)

OG: 1.080

Mash grain for 60 minutes at 152°F. Sparge and collect wort. Bring to a boil and add 3 1/2 cups corn syrup and 1 1/2 ounce Saaz hops. Boil for 90 minutes adding 1/2 ounce Saaz hops during the final 5 minutes. Cool wort and pitch yeast. Ferment at 70°F for 5 to 7 days. Transfer to a secondary fermenter, and condition an additional 7 to 10 days. Bottle, using 1/4 cup corn syrup, or keg. Age 10 to 14 days before serving.

# SQUARED CIRCLE E.S.B.

**W**hat is the best sport in the world to watch while you're drinking homebrew? Hands down, the answer has to be professional wrestling! Macho Man Randy Savage, Rowdy Roddy Piper, Lex Lugar, and the greatest of them all, Nature Boy Ric Flair. This is one we brew up for every pay-per-view wrestling event. So brew this up, and turn on wrestling. And should you not get hooked by the greatest show on earth, at least you'll have a lot of great beer.

7 1/2 POUNDS PALE 2-ROW MARIS OTTER MALT

1 POUND CRYSTAL MALT (40L)

1 POUND DEWOLF 2-ROW CARA-PILS MALT

1 POUND WHEAT MALT

1 1/2 OUNCES CHALLENGER HOPS, 7%

1 1/2 OUNCES AMERICAN FUGGLES HOPS

2 TEASPOONS GYPSUM

1 TEASPOON IRISH MOSS

WYEAST 1056 AMERICAN ALE YEAST

OG: 1.044

**M**ash grains for 60 minutes at 155°F. Add gypsum to the mash. Sparge and collect wort. Bring wort to a boil, and add Challenger hops. Boil 90 minutes, adding Fuggles hops after 80 minutes. Cool wort and pitch yeast. Ferment for 5 to 7 days. Transfer to a secondary fermenter, and cool to 55°F. Condition for 5 to 7 days. Bottle or keg. Age 3 to 5 days before serving.

# SWORD OF GOD
# BARLEYWINE

**A**t an original gravity of 1.200, this packs more than a little kick. Drink more than four of these in one night, and you'll feel the wrath of Michael, the archangel of death. Grab another one of these, and then reach for the sword of God.

19 POUNDS PALE 2-ROW MARIS OTTER MALT

2 POUNDS GOLDEN PROMISE MALT

1 POUND CRYSTAL MALT (20L)

4 OUNCES GALENA HOPS, 11%

2 1/2 OUNCES CHALLENGER HOPS

2 TEASPOONS GYPSUM

WYEAST 1056 AMERICAN ALE YEAST (STEPPED UP AT LEAST TWICE)

OG: 1.200

**M**ash grain for 60 minutes at 156°F. Add gypsum to mash. Sparge and collect wort. Bring wort to a boil, and add Galena hops. Boil for 90 minutes, adding Challenger hops after 85 minutes. Pitch yeast at 65°F and let rise naturally to 70°F. Ferment for 7 to 10 days. Transfer to a secondary fermenter, and cool to 60°F. Condition for 21 to 28 days. Bottle or keg. Age a minimum of 1 year before serving.

# OLDE ENOUGH TO KNOW BETTER

**O**ld ales, with their warm, malty character, make ideal winter beers. But be sure to plan ahead. If you'd like to have this beer for the Christmas season, you have to brew it in the middle of September, when summer is just ending and Christmas is the last thing on your mind. But remember that old ales get their name from the long aging process they require. Good things come to those who wait.

11 3/4 POUNDS PALE 2-ROW BRITISH MALT

1 POUND CRYSTAL MALT (80L)

1 POUND TORREFIED WHEAT

1/2 POUND PEATED MALT

1 POUND DARK BROWN SUGAR

1 OUNCE FUGGLES HOPS, 4.5%

1/2 OUNCE FUGGLES HOPS, 4.5%

WYEAST 1275 THAMES VALLEY ALE YEAST

OG: 1.069

**M**ash grains for 60 minutes at 155°F. Add gypsum to mash. Sparge and collect wort. Bring wort to a boil, and add 1 ounce Fuggles hops. Boil 120 minutes. Remove from heat and add 1/2 ounce Fuggles hops. Let steep for 15 minutes. Cool wort and pitch yeast. Ferment for 7 to 10 days. Transfer to a secondary fermenter, and cool to 55°F. Condition for 14 to 21 days. Bottle or keg. Age at least 2 months before serving.

# HORNY AS HELL
# OYSTER STOUT

**O**ysters have traditionally been known as one of nature's great aphrodisiacs. And though it's not as well known, stout is also considered a great aphrodisiac in many parts of the world. You can imagine what could happen if you combine the two! Oyster stout is very popular in the United Kingdom and is made using oyster essence. Since oyster essence is hard to come by, we've used whole oysters. And even if neither is a true aphrodisiac, a hearty stout is a great complement to oysters, as witnessed by Galway's annual fall oyster festival. So brew this beer, buy some oysters, buy some rubbers, and have fun!

8 POUNDS PALE 2-ROW BRITISH MALT

I POUND CRYSTAL MALT (120L)

I POUND TORREFIED WHEAT

3/4 POUND CHOCOLATE MALT

3/4 POUND ROASTED BARLEY

3/4 OUNCE FUGGLES HOPS

1/2 OUNCE FUGGLES HOPS

12 OYSTERS IN SHELL

I TEASPOON GYPSUM

WYEAST 1084 IRISH ALE YEAST

OG: 1.047

**M**ash grain for 60 minutes at 156°F. Sparge and collect wort. Bring wort to a boil, and add 3/4 ounce Fuggles hops. Boil for 90 minutes. Add the oysters (which have been placed in a hop bag) after 60 minutes and 1/2 ounce Fuggles hops after 85 minutes. Remove the bag with the oysters (and eat the oysters while you cool the wort). Pitch yeast at 60°F and let rise naturally to 68°F. Ferment for 5 to 7 days. Transfer to a secondary fermenter, and cool to 55°F. Condition for 3 to 5 days. Bottle or keg. Age 3 to 5 days before serving.

## ANASTASIA'S LAST BEER

The animated version of *Anastasia* was a wonderful work of fiction, but it wasn't quite how it happened. Czar Nicholas and his family were big fans of the British-style beer that has become known as Russian imperial stout. Just minutes before they were murdered the Romanov family toasted each other with glasses of beer. When their bodies were searched, the only thing found in Czar Nicholas's pocket was this beer recipe—the recipe for the beer they shared just before their death. Is this a true story? Maybe. But since no one knows what really happened, it's as good as any of the others.

15 POUNDS PALE 2-ROW BRITISH MALT

1 POUND CRYSTAL MALT (120L)

1 1/2 POUNDS MUNICH MALT

1 POUND CARA-PILS MALT

1 POUND TORREFIED WHEAT

1 POUND CHOCOLATE MALT

1 POUND ROASTED BARLEY

1/2 POUND FLAKED BARLEY

1 TEASPOON GYPSUM

4 OUNCES PERLE HOPS, 6.5%

4 OUNCES WILLAMETTE HOPS

WYEAST 1098 BRITISH ALE YEAST (STEPPED UP TWICE)

Fill a hop tea chamber with 4 ounces Willamette hops and steep at 175°F. Mash grains for 60 minutes at 156°F. Add gypsum to mash. Sparge and collect wort. Bring wort to a boil, and add 4 ounces Perle hops. Boil 90 minutes. Run hot wort through hop tea chamber. Cool wort and pitch yeast. Ferment for 7 to 10 days. Transfer to a secondary fermenter, and cool to 55°F. Condition for an additional 28 to 35 days. Bottle or keg. Age 4 to 6 months before serving.

## DRUNK AGAIN ON CHRISTMAS EVE WINTER WARMER

There are two things we love most about the Christmas season. One is that we can make and drink winter warmers. The other is that we can put on our favorite Christmas album—*Merle Haggard's Christmas*. The album includes classics like "Daddy's Drunk Again on Christmas Eve" and "Bobby's Not Getting a Puppy Again This Christmas." Brew this up, drink nine or ten, and put on Merle's album. Christmas will never be the same again.

11 POUNDS PALE 2-ROW MARIS OTTER MALT

1 POUND CRYSTAL MALT (80L)

1 POUND CARAMEL MALT

3/4 POUND CHOCOLATE MALT

1 POUND DARK BROWN SUGAR

1/2 POUND BUCKWHEAT HONEY

1 OUNCE BULLION HOPS, 9%

1 OUNCE DWARF TARGET HOPS

2 TEASPOONS GYPSUM

1/8 OUNCE CLOVES

1 CINNAMON STICK

1/2 TEASPOON MACE

WYEAST 1742 SWEDISH PORTER YEAST

---

OG: 1.065

---

**M**ash grain for 60 minutes at 156°F. Add gypsum to mash. Sparge and collect wort. Bring wort to a boil and add Bullion hops, honey, brown sugar, cloves, cinnamon, and mace. Boil for 90 minutes, adding Dwarf Target hops after 85 minutes. Pitch yeast at 65°F and let rise naturally to 72°F. Ferment for 5 to 7 days. Transfer to a secondary fermenter, and cool to 60°F. Condition for 7 to 10 days. Bottle or keg. Age 3 to 5 days before serving.

## HIGH P.A.

**N**o, this recipe is not against the law. Witness Great American Beer Festival medal winner Hempen Ale, which inspired this recipe. How you get the "special ingredient" is up to you. And should you be arrested acquiring it, don't call us, we don't know anything.

10 POUNDS PALE 2-ROW BRITISH MALT

1 POUND CRYSTAL MALT (60L)

1 1/2 POUNDS MUNICH MALT

1 POUND TORREFIED WHEAT

2 OUNCES CHALLENGER HOPS, 7%

1 OUNCE PERLE HOPS, 6.5%

2 OUNCES CASCADE HOPS (AROMA)

1 OUNCE HEMP SEEDS (WHOLE)

2 TEASPOONS GYPSUM

2 TEASPOONS IRISH MOSS

WYEAST 1056 AMERICAN ALE YEAST

---

OG: 1.060

---

Fill a hop tea chamber with 2 ounces Cascade hops and steep at 175°F. Mash grains for 60 minutes at 156°F. Add gypsum to mash. Sparge and collect wort. Bring wort to a boil, and add Challenger hops and Perle hops. Boil 90 minutes, adding the Irish moss after 85 minutes. Run hot wort through the hop tea chamber. Cool wort and pitch yeast. Ferment for 5 to 7 days. Transfer to a secondary fermenter, and cool to 55°F. Add hemp seeds. Condition for an additional 7 to 10 days. Bottle or keg. Age 7 to 10 days before serving.

# YORKSHIRE BITTER

**Y**ou've heard of Yorkshire pudding. Well, now you'll know Yorkshire bitter just as well. Yorkshire bitter is a golden ale with a smoother mouthfeel from the softer water. If you don't have soft water, buy 7 gallons of spring water to brew this beer.

6 POUNDS PALE 2-ROW BRITISH MALT

1 POUND CRYSTAL MALT (20L)

2 POUNDS TORREFIED WHEAT

1 TEASPOON GYPSUM

1 OUNCE EAST KENT GOLDINGS HOPS, 5%

2 OUNCES FUGGLES HOPS, 4.5%

2 TEASPOONS IRISH MOSS

WYEAST 1028 LONDON ALE YEAST

---

OG: 1.036

---

**M**ash grains for 60 minutes at 155°F. Add gypsum to the mash. Sparge and collect wort. Bring wort to a boil and add East Kent Goldings hops. Boil 90 minutes, adding 1 ounce Fuggles hops and Irish moss after 85 minutes. Remove from heat and add 1 ounce of Fuggles hops. Steep for 15 minutes. Cool wort and pitch yeast. Ferment for 5 to 7 days. Transfer to a secondary fermenter, and cool to 55°F. Condition for 7 to 10 days. Bottle or keg. Age 7 to 10 days before serving.

# Got a Little Irish in Ya?

**D**ry Irish stout is one of the classic styles of the world—black in color, with rich, smooth malt flavor and a creamy tan head. Unfortunately, some people find this intimidating and assume that stouts are a high-alcohol beer. In fact, Guinness, the standard for the style, is lower in alcohol than Budweiser. So put your fears aside and brew this up.

6 3/4 POUNDS PALE 2-ROW BRITISH MALT

1 POUND CRYSTAL MALT (120L)

1 POUND TORREFIED WHEAT

1 POUND FLAKED BARLEY

1 POUND ROASTED BARLEY

1 TEASPOON GYPSUM

1 OUNCE EAST KENT GOLDINGS HOPS, 5%

1/2 OUNCE FUGGLES HOPS, 4.5%

WYEAST 1084 IRISH ALE YEAST

OG: 1.040

**M**ash grains for 60 minutes at 155°F. Add gypsum to mash. Sparge and collect wort. Bring wort to a boil and add East Kent Goldings hops. Boil 90 minutes, adding Fuggles hops after 85 minutes. Cool wort and pitch yeast. Ferment for 5 to 7 days. Transfer to a secondary fermenter, and cool to 55°F. Condition for 7 to 10 days. Bottle or keg. Age 7 to 10 days before serving.

# OAT OF THIS
# WORLD STOUT

**O**ats. They're not just for breakfast anymore. Once you put them in this stout, we can guarantee that you'll find it a crime against God to waste good oats in morning oatmeal—unless, of course, you use one of these beers instead of water to make your morning oatmeal.

8 POUNDS PALE 2-ROW BRITISH MALT

1 POUND CRYSTAL MALT (80L)

1 POUND MUNICH MALT

1/2 POUND UNMALTED WHEAT

1 1/2 POUNDS ROLLED OATS

1 OUNCE CHALLENGER HOPS, 7%

1 1/2 OUNCES CASCADE HOPS

2 TEASPOONS GYPSUM

1 TEASPOON IRISH MOSS

WYEAST 1084 IRISH ALE YEAST

OG: 1.051

**P**lace oatmeal and 1 1/2 pounds 2-row malt in a pot. Add enough water to cover by 1 inch. Heat to 132°F and hold for 30 minutes. Raise temperature and bring to a boil. Remove from heat and cool to 152°F. Add remaining grain to mash tun. Then add oat/barley mixture. Mash grains for 60 minutes at 155°F. Add gypsum to mash. Sparge and collect wort. Bring wort to a boil, and add Challenger hops. Boil 90 minutes, adding Cascade hops after 80 minutes. Cool wort and pitch yeast. Ferment for 5 to 7 days. Transfer to a secondary fermenter, and cool to 55°F. Condition for 7 to 10 days. Bottle or keg. Age 5 to 7 days before serving.

# DEGENERATION X-TRA SPECIAL BITTER

**L**eave it to pro wrestling to produce a group of athletes who celebrate and promote degenerate behavior. And really, aren't all of us who choose to make alcohol our hobby a bit degenerate? This one is for Shawn Michaels, Hunter Hearst Helmsley, Chyna, X-Pac and the New Age Outlaws—and for all of us who say "The hell with it, let's just have fun." Suck it down!

8 POUNDS PALE 2-ROW MALT

1 POUND CRYSTAL MALT (80L)

1 POUND TORREFIED WHEAT

1 1/2 POUNDS DARK CORN SYRUP

1 1/2 OUNCES EAST KENT GOLDINGS HOPS

1 OUNCE CASCADE HOPS

2 OUNCES FUGGLE HOPS

1 TEASPOON GYPSUM

1 TEASPOON IRISH MOSS

BRITISH ALE YEAST

OG: 1.49

**M**ash grains for 60 minutes. Sprinkle gypsum on top of mash bed, sparge and collect wort. Boil for 90 minutes, adding corn syrup, East Kent Goldings hops, and Cascade hops at the beginning of the boil, 1 ounce Fuggle hops after 60 minutes, and 1 ounce Fuggle hops and Irish moss after 85 minutes. Cool wort and pitch yeast. Ferment at 68°F for 5 to 7 days. Transfer to a secondary fermenter and ferment an additional 3 days. Cool to 50°F and ferment an additional 2 days. Bottle or keg. Age 5 to 7 days before serving.

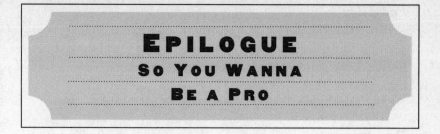

# EPILOGUE
## SO YOU WANNA
## BE A PRO

Ever dreamed of turning your hobby into a career? Each of the following professional brewers made the leap from neophyte to master, so we asked for their advice on pursuing a brewing career. All agreed that homebrewing experience is an asset, although a few felt that formal education at a facility like the University of California at Davis or the Siebel Institute helps to set you apart from the crowd.

### Greg Noonan
Do it. The worst thing that can happen to this industry is that homebrewers stop being the engine that drives it. When it becomes filled with school-trained brewers who brew because it is a stable career and not for a love of beer, that's when craft brew stops being what it is today.

### Michael Ferguson
Persevere. Volunteer to help around your local brewery. Don't tell them you want to be a brewer, but offer to shovel out the mash or clean tanks. And most important, always be the last one to leave.

### Don Gortemiller
Homebrewing is definitely an asset. It's just a question of scale. The process isn't that much different. Or you could win the lottery.

### Fal Allen

Bring homebrew to the brewery where you'd like to work. It's your portfolio that shows you know how to make good beer. I always have people coming in looking for brewing jobs, but none of them ever brings me samples.

### Dan Rogers

Take some classes. And if you can, become a partner in your own brewery.

### Dick Cantwell

Create a homebrew portfolio. Brew a lot of different styles to show that you have a grasp on a wide range of beers.

### Ray McNeill

Read a lot. Practice a lot. And get a job in a real brewery doing whatever you can.

### Paul Sayler

Get your foot in the door. Volunteer to help out doing whatever is needed. And until someone gives you a chance, brew a lot and read as much literature as you can.

### Drew Cluley

Perfect one or two styles, and use those as your resumé. It's important to show people that you know how to brew and that you understand beer and the brewing process.

### Bill Owens

Nowadays, you really need some formal education. Enroll in one of the courses at one of the brewing schools.

*Nick Hankin and Luca Evans*

Choose one style and brew it over and over until you can re-create it the exact same way every time. In a professional brewery, that's what you're going to have to do. Also, make yourself known among your local brewing community, and let them know you'd like to become a pro.

# APPENDIX A
## EQUIPMENT UPGRADES

### HOP TEA CHAMBER

Capture hop flavor and aroma without imparting bitterness by adding hop tea to your fermented wort. Place leaf hops in a hop bag or stainless steel basket, and steep them in a sealed insulated jug with 1/2 gallon of 160°F water for 2 to 4 hours. Add the tea to your wort prior to cooling.

An additional option is to run your entire batch of hot wort through the leaves in the basket as you drain the hop tea. Collect the wort in another brew pot or plastic bucket, and then cool with your wort chiller as normal.

To make the stainless steel basket, cut a rectangle of stainless window screen that measures 22 inches by 7 inches (for a 7-inch diameter jug). Then cut a circle that is just under 7 inches in diameter. Roll the rectangle to form a tube, and fasten together with stainless wire. Attach the circle to the bottom of the tube in a similar manner, and you have your hop basket. (See Figures 1 and 2.)

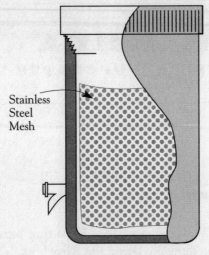

Stainless
Steel
Mesh

1-GALLON INSULATED JUG

FIGURE 1. HOP TEA CHAMBER

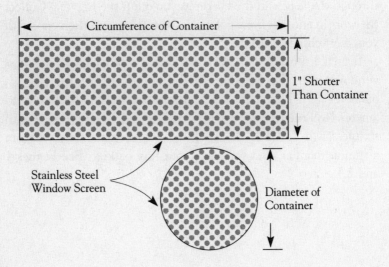

Circumference of Container

1" Shorter
Than Container

Stainless Steel
Window Screen

Diameter of
Container

FIGURE 2. HOP LEAF BASKET

## CORNI KEG TO A CASK

The standard Cornelius keg can be easily converted into a Corni cask. The Corni cask differs from the Corni keg in that the cask is laid on its side to increase the surface area for yeast sedimentation. You will need to cut down the beer tube in the keg to a length of about 3 inches. A screen placed over the cask's beer outlet port prevents any hops that may have been used from blocking the port or turning up in your pint. (See Figure 3.) The angle and tilt of the cask must be fine-tuned to minimize disturbing cask sediment during serving.

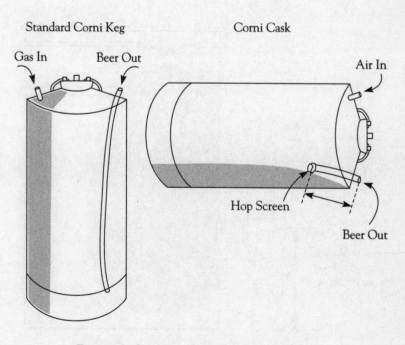

Standard Corni Keg      Corni Cask

Gas In     Beer Out

Air In

Hop Screen

Beer Out

FIGURE 3. CORNELIUS CASK MODIFICATIONS

Bottling spigots are readily available at homebrew supply stores. These valves come with a threaded end that fits inside the bucket and a plastic nut with rubber washers to make a seal. Cut a hole (about 3/4 inch in diameter or whatever suits the threaded end of your valve) one-third of the way up the plastic fermenting bucket. (See Figure 4.) This will allow you to take samples from the middle of your fermenting beer without disturbing the yeast head and, more important, without exposing your beer to potential contamination when you remove the lid. This is especially important when making cask beers, since you'll want to check gravity every day, if not a couple of times per day. Make sure to disassemble the valve and thoroughly sanitize all the parts before you brew.

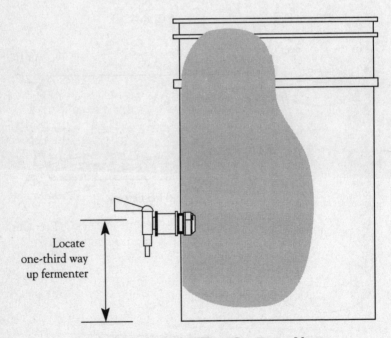

Locate one-third way up fermenter

FIGURE 4. FERMENTER WITH SAMPLING VALVE

## MINI-MASH TUN

Improve your extract brews with a partial mash. To get more from specialty grains than you do by steeping them, combine them with an equal weight of crushed pale malt in a mini-mash. Get two 1 1/2- to 2-gallon buckets. (Restaurants are a good source. Many of them get things like cole slaw and potato salad in food grade buckets. More than likely they'll be glad to give you their empties.) Hand-poke small holes (approximately 1/8 inch) in the bottom of one of them—as many as you can. (See Figure 5.) Set this inside the other bucket, and add your grains and about 3/4 gallon of 160°F water. Steep for at least 30 minutes, and add it to boiling extract wort. You can add a spigot to the bottom bucket for drainage or just lift out the perforated one. This technique allows you to control the water-to-grain ratio and improve extract and flavor.

## CARBOY UNION SYSTEM

A glass carboy is the most sanitary medium in which to ferment beer. Plastic fermenters are easily scratched, and these scratches can harbor bacteria, which can lead to infection.

Unfortunately, primary fermenting in a carboy makes it nearly impossible to harvest top-fermenting yeast for subsequent batches (unless you have *really* thin arms). The carboy union system is based on the Burton union system, made famous by the Bass Brewery. It will allow you to collect the freshest, most viable yeast while still using glass for your fermenter.

Transfer your wort into the carboy, filling it to the bottom of the neck of the bottle. Pitch your yeast and aerate well. Attach a drilled rubber stopper fitted with a 3-foot piece of sanitized rubber hose. Place the end in a bucket of diluted iodophor solution. Allow the beer to expel krausen for 2 to 3 hours, to let some residual proteins and hops resins be expelled.

Sanitize another carboy, and affix a well-sanitized "fermacap,"

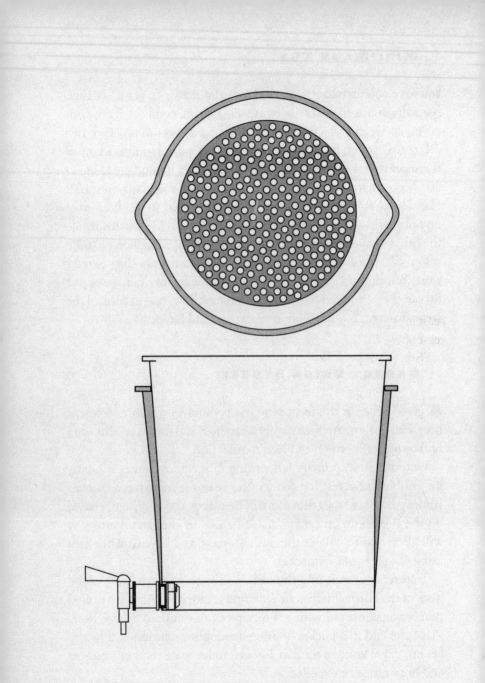

Figure 5. Mini Mash Tun

which is a carboy cap fitted with two openings. Affix a sanitized air-lock to one of the openings. Remove the hose from the bucket, rinsing the end well with iodophor solution. Then attach to the fermacap opening. (See Figure 6.)

Collect about 1 cup of yeast, and then brew and pitch fresh wort onto the collected yeast. If you don't plan to brew right away, affix a solid rubber stopper on the carboy, and place it in the refrigerator as near to freezing as possible, but *not* freezing. The refrigerated yeast should stay viable for 7 to 10 days.

The first couple of times you do this, you may want to decant the collected yeast into a sterilized glass measuring cup to get an idea of what 1 cup of yeast looks like. Discard the remaining yeast in the carboy, and clean and sanitize before adding the harvested yeast. After a couple of times doing this, you should be able to eyeball 1 cup of yeast in the carboy, which will allow you to eliminate transferring the yeast and exposing it to possible contamination.

This system works for top-fermenting or top-cropping yeast only. Don't try it with a bottom-fermenting or lager yeast.

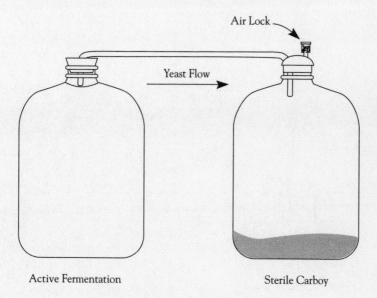

Air Lock

Yeast Flow

Active Fermentation

Sterile Carboy

FIGURE 6. CARBOY UNION SYSTEM

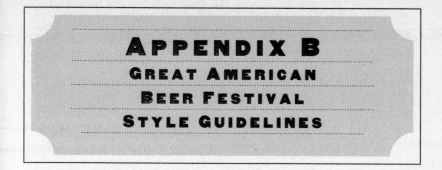

In our last book, we included the style guidelines for the American Homebrewers Association. This time, we thought we would give you the standards that the pros are held up to when they compete.

## NONLAGERS

### Classic English-Style Pale Ale

Classic English pale ales are golden to copper colored and display English-variety hop character. High hop bitterness, flavor, and aroma should be evident. This medium-bodied pale ale has low to medium maltiness. Low caramel is allowable. Fruity-ester flavors and aromas are moderate to strong. Chill haze is allowable at cold temperatures. Diacetyl (butterscotch character) should be at very low levels or not perceived at all.

### India Pale Ale

India pale ales are characterized by intense hop bitterness with a high alcohol content. A high hopping rate and the use of water with high mineral content result in a crisp, dry beer. This golden to deep copper-colored ale has a full, flowery hop aroma and may have a strong hop flavor (in addition to the hop bitterness). India pale ales possess medium maltiness and body. Fruity-ester flavors and aromas are moderate to very strong. Chill haze is allowable at cold temperatures.

### American Pale Ale

American pale ales range from golden to light copper in color. The style is characterized by American-variety hops used to produce high hop bitterness, flavor, and aroma. American pale ales have medium body and low to medium maltiness. Low caramel character is allowable. Fruity-ester flavor and aroma should be moderate to strong. Diacetyl should be absent or present at very low levels. Chill haze is allowable at cold temperatures.

### American Amber Ale

American amber ales range from light copper to light brown in color. They are characterized by American-variety hops used to produce high hop bitterness, flavor, and aroma. Amber ales have medium to high maltiness, with medium to low caramel character. They should have medium body. The style may have low levels of fruity-ester flavor and aroma. Diacetyl should be absent or barely perceived. Chill haze is allowable at cold temperatures.

### Traditional English-Style Bitters

English bitters range from golden to copper in color and are well attenuated. Good hop character and mild carbonation traditionally characterize draught-cask versions. Bottled versions may have a slight increase in carbon dioxide content in all three subcategories. Fruity-ester character and very low diacetyl (butterscotch) character are acceptable in aroma and flavor. Chill haze is allowable at cold temperatures.

English-Style Ordinary Bitter: Ordinary bitter is gold to copper colored with medium bitterness, light to medium body, and low to medium residual malt sweetness. Diacetyl and fruity-ester properties should be minimized in this form of bitter.

English-Style Special Bitter: Special bitters are more robust than ordinary bitters. They have medium body and medium residual sweetness. In addition, the special bitters have more hop character than ordinary bitters.

English-Style Extra Special Bitter: Extra special bitters possess medium to strong hop qualities in aroma, flavor, and bitterness. The residual malt sweetness of these richly flavored, full-bodied bitters is more pronounced than in other bitters.

## Scottish-Style Ales

Characterized by a rounded flavor profile, Scottish ales are malty, caramel-like, soft, and chewy. Hop rates are low. Yeast characters such as diacetyl (butterscotch) and sulfuriness are acceptable at very low levels. Scottish ales range from golden amber to deep brown in color and may possess a faint smoky character. Bottled versions of this traditional draught beer may contain higher amounts of carbon dioxide than is typical for draught versions. Chill haze is acceptable at low temperatures.

## Scottish-Style Light Ale

Scottish light ales represent the mildest form of this ale. Little bitterness is perceived. Scottish light ales are light bodied. Very low hop bitterness is acceptable, and hop flavor or aroma should not be perceived. Chill haze is acceptable at low temperatures.

Scottish-Style Heavy Ale: Scottish heavy ales are moderate in strength and dominated by a smooth, sweet maltiness balanced with low, but perceptible, hop bitterness. They have medium body, and fruity esters are very low, if evident. Chill haze is acceptable at low temperatures.

SCOTTISH-STYLE EXPORT ALE: Scottish export ales are sweet, caramel-like, and malty. Their bitterness is perceived as low to medium. They have medium body. Fruity-ester character may be apparent. Chill haze is acceptable at low temperatures.

GOLDEN ALE/CANADIAN-STYLE ALE: Golden ales and Canadian-style ales are a straw to golden-blonde variation of the classic American-style pale ale. However, a golden ale more closely approximates a lager in its crisp, dry palate, low (but noticeable) hop floral aroma, and light body. Perceived bitterness is low to medium. Fruity esters may be perceived but do not predominate. Chill haze should be absent.

KÖLSCH: Kölsch is warm fermented and aged at cold temperatures (German ale or Alt-style beer). It is characterized by a golden color and a slightly dry, winey, and subtly sweet palate. Caramel character should not be evident. The body is light. This beer has low hop flavor and aroma with medium bitterness. Wheat can be used in brewing this beer, which is fermented with ale or lager yeasts. Fruity esters should be minimally perceived, if at all. Chill haze should be absent or minimal.

## English-Style Brown Ales

ENGLISH-STYLE LIGHT MILD ALE: English-style light mild ales range from light amber to light brown in color. Malty sweet tones dominate the flavor profile, with little hop bitterness or flavor. Hop aroma can be light. Very low diacetyl flavors may be appropriate in this low-alcohol beer. Fruity-ester level is very low. Chill haze is allowable at cold temperatures.

ENGLISH-STYLE DARK MILD ALE: English-style dark mild ales range from deep copper to dark brown (often with a red tint) in color. Malty sweet, caramel, licorice, and roast malt tones dominate the flavor and aroma profile, with very little hop flavor or aroma. Very low diacetyl flavors may be appropriate in this low-alcohol beer. Fruity-ester level is very low.

ENGLISH-STYLE BROWN ALE: English-style brown ales range from deep copper to brown in color. They have a medium body, and a dry to sweet maltiness dominates with very little hop flavor or aroma. Fruity-ester flavors are appropriate. Diacetyl should be very low, if evident. Chill haze is allowable at cold temperatures.

## American Brown Ale

American brown ales look like their English brown ale counterparts but have an evident hop aroma and increased bitterness. They have medium body, and estery and fruity-ester characters should be subdued. Diacetyl should not be perceived. Chill haze is allowable at cold temperatures.

## German-Style Brown Ale/Düsseldorf-Style Altbier

Brown in color, this German ale may be highly hopped (though the 25–35 International Bitterness Units range is more normal for the majority of Altbiers from Düsseldorf) and has a medium body and malty flavor. A variety of malts, including wheat, may be used. Hop character may be evident in the flavor. The overall impression is clean, crisp, and flavorful. Fruity esters should be low. No diacetyl or chill haze should be perceived.

# German-Style Wheat Ales

BERLINER WEISSE: This is the lightest of all the German wheat beers. The unique combination of a yeast and lactic acid bacteria fermentation yields a beer that is acidic, highly attenuated, and very light bodied. The carbonation of a Berliner weisse is high, and hop rates are very low. Hop character should not be perceived. Fruity esters will be evident. No diacetyl should be perceived.

WEIZEN/WEISSBIER: The aroma and flavor of a weissbier are decidedly fruity and phenolic. The phenolic characteristics are often described as clove- or nutmeg-like and can be smoky or even vanilla-like. These beers are made with at least 50 percent malted wheat, and hop rates are quite low. Weissbier is well attenuated and very highly carbonated, yet its relatively high starting gravity and alcohol content make it a medium- to full-bodied beer. Banana-like esters are often present. If yeast is present, the beer will appropriately have yeast flavor and a characteristically fuller mouthfeel. No diacetyl should be perceived.

DUNKEL WEIZEN/DUNKEL WEISSBIER: This beer style is characterized by a distinct sweet maltiness, and roasted malt and chocolate-like character, but the estery and phenolic elements of a pale weissbier still prevail. Color can range from copper-brown to dark brown. Carbonation and hop bitterness are similar to a pale South German–style weissbier. Usually dark barley malts are used in conjunction with dark cara or color malts, and the percentage of wheat malt is at least 50 percent. No diacetyl should be perceived.

WEIZENBOCK/WEISSBOCK: This style can be pale or dark and, like a bottom-fermented bock, has a high starting gravity and alcohol content. Its malty sweetness is balanced with a clovelike phenolic and fruity-estery banana element to produce a well-rounded aroma and flavor. As is true with all other German wheat beers, hop rates are low and carbonation is high. It has a medium to full body. If dark, a mild roast malt character should emerge in flavor and, to a lesser degree, in the aroma. No diacetyl should be perceived.

### Robust Porter

Robust porters are black in color and have a roast malt flavor but no roasted barley flavor. They have a sharp bitterness of black malt without a highly burned or charcoal flavor. Robust porters range from a medium to full body and have a malty sweetness. Hop bitterness is medium to high, with hop aroma and flavor ranging from negligible to medium. Fruity esters should be evident in proportional balance with roast malt and hop bitterness character.

### Brown Porter

Brown porters are mid- to dark brown (may have red tint) in color. No roasted barley or strong burned malt character should be perceived. Low to medium malt sweetness is acceptable, along with medium hop bitterness. This is a light- to medium-bodied beer. Fruity esters are acceptable. Hop flavor and aroma may vary from being negligible to medium in character.

### Dry Stouts

CLASSIC IRISH-STYLE DRY STOUT: Dry stouts have an initial malt and caramel flavor profile with a distinctive dry-roasted bitterness in the finish. They achieve a dry-roasted character through the use of roasted barley. Some slight acidity may be perceived but is not necessary. Hop aroma and flavor should not be perceived. Dry stouts have medium body. Fruity esters are minimal and overshadowed by malt, hop bitterness, and roasted barley character. Diacetyl (butterscotch) should be very low or not perceived. Head retention and rich character should be part of its visual character.

FOREIGN-STYLE STOUT: Like classic dry stouts, foreign-style stouts have an initial malt sweetness and caramel flavor with a distinctive dry-roasted bitterness in the finish. Some slight acidity is permissible, and a medium- to full-bodied mouthfeel is appropriate. Hop aroma and flavor should not be perceived. The perception of fruity esters is low. Diacetyl (butterscotch) should be negligible or not perceived. Head retention is excellent.

## Specialty Stouts

SWEET STOUT: Sweet stouts, also referred to as cream stouts, have less roasted bitter flavor and more full-bodied mouthfeel than dry stouts. The style can be given more body with milk sugar (lactose) before bottling. Malt sweetness and chocolate and caramel flavor should dominate the flavor profile. Hops should balance sweetness without contributing apparent flavor or aroma.

OATMEAL STOUT: Oatmeal stouts typically include oatmeal in their grist, resulting in a pleasant, full flavor and smooth profile that is rich without being grainy. Roasted malt character of caramel and chocolate should be evident, smooth, and not bitter. Bitterness is moderate, not high. Hop flavor and aroma are optional but should not overpower the overall balance. This is a medium- to full-bodied beer, with minimal fruity esters.

## Strong Ales

ENGLISH OLD ALE/STRONG ALE: Amber to copper in color, English strong ales are medium to full bodied with a malty sweetness. Fruity-ester flavor and aroma should contribute to the character of this ale. Bitterness should be evident and balanced with malt and/or caramel sweetness. Alcohol types can be varied and complex. Chill haze is acceptable at low temperatures.

STRONG "SCOTCH" ALE: Scotch ales are overwhelmingly malty and full bodied. Perception of hop bitterness is very low. Hop flavor and aroma are very low or nonexistent. Color ranges from deep copper to brown. The clean alcohol flavor balances the rich and dominant sweet maltiness in flavor and aroma. A caramel character is often part of the profile. Fruity esters are generally at medium aromatic and flavor levels. A peaty or smoky character may be evident at low levels. Low diacetyl levels are acceptable. Chill haze is allowable at cold temperatures.

IMPERIAL STOUT: Dark copper to very black, imperial stouts typically have an alcohol content exceeding 8 percent. The extremely rich malty flavor and aroma are balanced with assertive hopping and fruity-ester characteristics. Perceived bitterness can be moderate and balanced with malt character to very high in the darker versions. Roasted malt astringency and bitterness can be moderately perceived but should not overwhelm the overall character. Hop aroma can be subtle to overwhelmingly floral. Diacetyl (butterscotch) levels should be very low.

OTHER STRONG ALES: Any style of beer can be made stronger than the classic style guidelines. The goal should be to reach a balance between the style's character and the additional alcohol.

### Barleywine

Barleywines range from tawny copper to dark brown in color and have a full body and high residual malty sweetness. Complexity of alcohols and fruity-ester characters are often high and counterbalanced by the perception of low to assertive bitterness and extraordinary alcohol content. Hop aroma and flavor may be minimal to very high. Diacetyl should be very low. A caramel and vinous aroma and flavor are part of the character. Chill haze is allowable at cold temperatures.

# Belgian-Style Ales

BELGIAN-STYLE DUBBEL: This medium- to full-bodied, dark amber- to brown-colored ale has a malty sweetness and nutty, chocolate, roast malt aroma. A faint hop aroma is acceptable. Dubbels are also characterized by low bitterness and no hop flavor. Very small quantities of diacetyl are acceptable. Fruity esters (especially banana) are appropriate at low levels. Head retention is dense and moussy.

BELGIAN-STYLE TRIPPEL: Trippels are often characterized by a spicy, phenolic-clove flavor. A banana fruity ester is also common. These pale or light-colored ales usually finish sweet. The beer is characteristically medium to full bodied, with a neutral hop-to-malt balance. Low hop flavor is okay. Alcohol strength and flavor should be perceived.

BELGIAN-STYLE PALE ALE: Belgian-style pale ales are characterized by low but noticeable hop bitterness, flavor, and aroma. Light to medium body and low malt aroma are typical. They are golden to deep amber in color. Noble-type hops are commonly used. Low to medium fruity esters are evident in aroma and flavor. Low caramel or toasted malt flavor is okay. Diacetyl should not be perceived. Chill haze is allowable at cold temperatures.

BELGIAN-STYLE STRONG ALE: Belgian-style strong ales are often vinous, with darker styles typically colored with dark candy sugar. The perception of hop bitterness can vary from low to high, and hop aroma and flavor are very low. These beers are highly attenuated and have a highly alcoholic character, being medium bodied rather than full bodied. Very little or no diacetyl is perceived. Chill haze is allowable at cold temperatures.

## *Belgian-Style Specialty Ales*

BELGIAN-STYLE FLANDERS BROWN ALE/OUD BRUIN ALE: This light- to medium-bodied deep copper to brown ale is characterized by a slight vinegar or lactic sourness and spiciness. A fruity-estery character is apparent, with no hop flavor or aroma. Flanders brown ales have low to medium bitterness. Very small quantities of diacetyl are acceptable. Roasted malt character in aroma and flavor is acceptable at low levels.

BELGIAN-STYLE WHITE (OR WIT): Belgian white ales are brewed using unmalted and/or malted wheat and malted barley and can be spiced with coriander and orange peel. These very pale beers are typically cloudy. The style is further characterized by the use of noble-type hops to achieve a low to medium bitterness and hop flavor. These dry beers have low to medium body, no diacetyl, and a low fruity-ester content.

BELGIAN-STYLE LAMBIC: Unblended, naturally fermented lambic is intensely estery, sour, and acetic flavored. Low in carbon dioxide, these hazy beers are brewed with unmalted wheat and malted barley. They are very low in hop bitterness. Cloudiness is acceptable. These beers are quite dry and light bodied.

BELGIAN-STYLE GUEUZE LAMBIC: These unflavored blended and secondary fermented lambic beers may be very dry or mildly sweet and are characterized by intensely fruity-estery, sour, and acidic flavors. These pale beers are brewed with unmalted wheat, malted barley, and stale, aged hops. They are very low in hop bitterness. Cloudiness is acceptable. These beers are quite dry and light bodied.

BELGIAN-STYLE FRUIT LAMBIC: These beers, also known by the names *framboise*, *kriek*, *pêche*, and others, are characterized by fruit flavors and aromas. The intense color reflects the choice of fruit. Sourness predominates the flavor profile. They may be very dry or mildly sweet. Please specify the type of fruit used when registering your beer.

## LAGERS

### European-Style Pilsners

GERMAN-STYLE PILSNER: A classic German pilsner has a very light straw or golden color and is well hopped. Hop bitterness is high. Hop aroma and flavor are moderate and quite obvious. It is a well-attenuated, medium-bodied beer, but a malty accent can be perceived. Fruity esters and diacetyl should not be perceived. There should be no chill haze. Its head should be dense and rich.

BOHEMIAN-STYLE PILSNER: Pilsners in this subcategory are similar to German pilsners; however, they are slightly more full bodied and can be as dark as light amber. This style balances moderate bitterness and noble-type hop aroma and flavor with a malty, slightly sweet medium body. Diacetyl may be perceived in very low amounts. There should be no chill haze. Its head should be dense and rich.

CONTINENTAL-STYLE PILSNER: Continental pilsners are straw to golden in color and are well-attenuated beers. This medium-bodied beer is often brewed with rice, corn, wheat, or other grain or sugar adjuncts making up part of the mash. Fruity esters and diacetyl should not be perceived. There should be no chill haze.

### Münchener Helles and Export

MÜNCHENER HELLES: This beer has a relatively low bitterness. It is a medium-bodied, malt-emphasized beer; however, certain versions can approach a balance of hop character and maltiness. There should not be any caramel character. Color is light straw to golden. Fruity esters and diacetyl should not be perceived.

DORTMUNDER/EXPORT: Both starting gravity and medium bitterness are somewhat higher than a Münchener Helles. Hop flavor and aroma are perceptible but low. The color of this style may be slightly darker, and the body will be fuller but still medium bodied. Fruity esters, chill haze, and diacetyl should not be perceived.

### American Light Lager

According to U.S. Food and Drug Administration regulations, when used in reference to caloric content, "light" beers must have at least 25 percent fewer calories than the "regular" version of that beer. Such beers must have certain analysis data printed on the package label. These beers are extremely light colored, light in body, and high in carbonation. Flavor is mild and bitterness is very low. Chill haze, fruity esters, and diacetyl should be absent.

### American Lager

Very light in body and color, American lagers are clean, crisp, and aggressively carbonated. Malt sweetness is absent. Corn, rice, or other grain or sugar adjuncts are often used. Hop aroma is absent. Hop bitterness is slight, and hop flavor is mild or negligible. Chill haze, fruity esters, and diacetyl should be absent.

### American Premium Lager

Similar to the American lager, this style is a more flavorful, medium-bodied beer and should contain few or no adjuncts at all. Color may be deeper than the American lager, and alcohol content and bitterness may also be greater. Hop aroma and flavor are low or negligible. Chill haze, fruity esters, and diacetyl should be absent.

Some beers marketed as "premium" (based on price) may not fit this definition in this competition.

## American Specialty Lagers

AMERICAN DRY LAGER: This straw-colored lager lacks sweetness and is reminiscent of an American-style light lager. However, its starting gravity and alcoholic strength are greater. Hop rates are low, and carbonation is high. Chill haze, fruity esters, and diacetyl should be absent.

AMERICAN ICE LAGER: This style is slightly higher in alcohol than most other light-colored, American-style lagers. Its body is light to medium, and it has a low residual malt sweetness. It has few or no adjuncts. Color is very pale to golden. Hop bitterness is low but certainly perceptible. Hop aroma and flavor are low. Chill haze, fruity esters, and diacetyl should not be perceived. Typically these beers are chilled before filtration so that ice crystals (which may or may not be removed) are formed. This can contribute to a higher alcohol content (up to 0.5 percent more).

## American Malt Liquor

High in starting gravity and alcoholic strength, this style is somewhat diverse. Some American malt liquors are just slightly stronger than American lagers, and others approach bock strength. Some residual sweetness is perceived. Hop rates are very low, contributing little bitterness and virtually no hop aroma or flavor. Chill haze, diacetyl, and fruity esters should not be perceived.

## Amber Lagers

VIENNA LAGER: Beers in this category are reddish brown or copper colored. They are light to medium in body. The beer is characterized by malty aroma, slight malt sweetness, and clean hop bitterness. Noble-type hop aromas and flavors should be low to medium. Fruity esters, diacetyl, and chill haze should not be perceived.

AMERICAN AMBER LAGER: American-style amber lagers are amber, reddish-brown, or copper colored. They are medium bodied. There is a noticeable degree of caramel-type malt character in flavor and often in aroma. This is a broad subcategory in which the hop bitterness, flavor, and aroma may be accentuated or may be present at only relatively low levels yet noticeable. Fruity esters, diacetyl, and chill haze should be absent.

## Märzen/Oktoberfest

Märzen/Oktoberfests can range from golden to reddish brown. Sweet maltiness should dominate slightly over a clean, hop bitterness. Malt character should be toasted rather than strongly caramel. Hop aroma and flavor should be low but notable. Fruity esters are minimal, if perceived at all. Diacetyl and chill haze should not be perceived.

## Dark Lagers

EUROPEAN-STYLE DARK/MÜNCHENER DUNKEL: These beers have a pronounced malty aroma and flavor that dominates over the clean, crisp, moderate hop bitterness. A classic Münchener dunkel should have a chocolate-like, roast malt, breadlike aroma that comes from the use of Munich dark malt. Chocolate or roast malts can be used, but the percentage used should be minimal. Noble-type hop flavor and aroma should be low but perceptible. Diacetyl is acceptable at very low levels. Fruity esters and chill haze should not be perceived.

AMERICAN DARK LAGER: This beer's maltiness is less pronounced, and its body is light. Nonmalt adjuncts are often used, and hop rates are low. Hop bitterness flavor and aroma are low. Carbonation is high and more typical of an American-style light lager than a European dark lager. Fruity esters, diacetyl, and chill haze should not be perceived.

GERMAN-STYLE SCHWARZBIER: These beers have a roasted malt character without the associated bitterness. Malt flavor and aroma are low, as is sweetness. Hop bitterness is low to medium in character. Noble-type hop flavor and aroma should be low but perceptible. There should be no fruity esters. Diacetyl is acceptable at very low levels.

## Bocks

TRADITIONAL BOCK: Traditional bocks are made with all malt and are strong, malty, medium- to full-bodied, bottom-fermented beers with moderate hop bitterness that should increase proportionately with the starting gravity. Hop flavor should be low, and hop aroma should be very low. Bocks can range in color from deep copper to dark brown. Fruity esters may be perceived at low levels.

HELLES BOCK/MAIBOCK: The German word *hell* means "light colored," and as such, a helles bock is light in color. Maibocks are also light-colored bocks. The malty character should come through in the aroma and flavor. Body is medium to full. Hop bitterness should be low, and noble-type hop aroma and flavor may be at low to medium levels. Bitterness increases with gravity. Fruity esters should be minimal. Diacetyl levels should be very low. Chill haze should not be perceived.

DOPPELBOCK: Malty sweetness is dominant but should not be cloying. Doppelbocks are full bodied and deep amber to dark brown in color. Astringency from roast malts is absent. Alcoholic strength is high, and hop rates increase with gravity. Hop bitterness and flavor should be low and hop aroma absent. Fruity esters are commonly perceived but at low to moderate levels.

## HYBRID AND MIXED STYLES

### American Lager/Ale or Cream Ale

This mild, pale, light-bodied ale is made using a warm fermentation (top or bottom) and cold lagering or by blending top- and bottom-fermented beers. Hop bitterness and flavor are very low and hop aroma is often absent. Sometimes referred to as cream ales, these beers are crisp and refreshing.

### Smoke-Flavored Beers

BAMBERG-STYLE RAUCHBIER LAGER: Rauchbier should have a smoky character prevalent in the aroma and flavor. The beer is generally toasted malty sweet and full bodied with low to medium hop bitterness. Noble-type hop flavor is low but perceptible. Low noble-type hop aroma is optional. The aroma should strike a balance between malt, hop, and smoke. Fruity esters, diacetyl, and chill haze should not be perceived.

SMOKE-FLAVORED BEER (LAGER OR ALE): Any style of beer can be smoked. The goal is to reach a balance between the style's character and the smoky properties.

### Nonalcoholic Malt Beverages

Nonalcoholic malt beverages should emulate the character of a previously listed category or subcategory designation but without the alcohol (less than 0.5 percent).

# GENERAL INDEX

# Index of Brewers' Recipes